# QUANTUM WHISPERS

ALSO BY ROBERT T. YARBOROUGH

*Beyond Space and Time*

*Getting Down to Brass Tacks*

*The Outrage Paradox*

*The Self Coaching Blueprint*

*Be Done With It*

# QUANTUM WHISPERS

A Journey Into Co-Creation, Where Science Meets Spirit and Possibilities Are Infinite.

Robert T. Yarborough

Pranava Books

Publisher's Cataloging-in-Publication Data

Yarborough, Robert T., 1960–
Quantum Whispers: A Journey Into Co-Creation, Where Science Meets Spirit and Possibilities Are Infinite / Robert T. Yarborough.
—First edition.
p. cm.
ISBN 979-8-9912582-6-5

1. Spirituality. 2. Quantum physics—Religious aspects. 3. Personal growth. 4. Self-help techniques. 5. Metaphysics. I. Title.
BL624 .Y37 2025
204/.4 — dc23
LCCN: 2025901413

Printed in the United States of America
10 9 8 7 6 5 4 3 2 1

# Dedication

To my beloved children,
You are the stars that light my journey, the sparks of
wonder that keep my curiosity alive.


May you always look to the universe with awe, to yourselves with courage,
and to the unseen with trust. Never stop seeking, questioning, and dreaming,
for within you lies the same infinite potential that shapes the cosmos.


You are my greatest connection to the Divine.

# Table of Contents

# Author's Preface

*"Harmony is not something the universe strives for
—it is what the universe is"*

This book is not the work of a quantum physicist or even a lay expert in the field. I hold no advanced degrees in theoretical physics, nor do I spend my days immersed in complex equations that seek to decode the fabric of reality. What I am, however, is a passionate reader, a curious researcher, and an eternal seeker of the mysteries that define our universe—and our place within it.

The journey that led to this book began with a single question: How do science and spirituality intersect to shape the world we experience? Like many of you, I have often felt the pull of both the rational and the mystical. The questions that science seeks to answer often feel incomplete without the depth of meaning that spirituality provides. And yet, for too long, these domains have been treated as separate worlds, as though understanding one invalidates the other.

What I hope to accomplish in these pages is to bridge that perceived divide. Quantum mechanics, for all its complexity, reveals a universe that is dynamic, interconnected, and alive with potential. Similarly, the spiritual traditions that have guided humanity for millennia teach us that we are not separate from this universe but deeply embedded within it. When viewed together, they tell a story not only of atoms and energy but of intention, consciousness, and purpose.

This book is not a definitive guide to quantum theory, nor is it a theological treatise. Instead, it is an invitation—to explore, to reflect, and to wonder. It is for the thinkers and the dreamers, the skeptics and the believers, and anyone who has ever paused to marvel at the night sky and felt the undeniable tug of the infinite.

In writing this book, I have drawn from the work of brilliant scientists, philosophers, and spiritual teachers. Their insights have shaped my own understanding and are woven throughout these chapters. However, I have also sought to make these concepts accessible to those of us who are neither physicists nor theologians but who nonetheless feel compelled to engage with life's most profound questions.

If you take away one idea from these pages, let it be this: You are not a passive observer of the universe. Through your thoughts, intentions, and actions, you are an active participant in the unfolding of reality. The quantum field, with all its mysteries and potentialities, is not separate from you—it is within and around you, waiting for your engagement.

So, let us explore the quantum field and the soul, the fabric of the cosmos, and the essence of what it means to be human. Let us journey together into the space where science and spirituality meet and discover the profound truth that we are not only observers of the universe—we are co-creators within it.

—Robert T. Yarborough

January 2025

# Introduction

*"The cosmos is within us. We are made of star-stuff.
We are a way for the universe to know itself."*
— Carl Sagan

## A Quiet Moment of Wonder

A woman stands alone at dawn, her bare feet pressing into the cool, damp earth. The horizon glows faintly, a brushstroke of amber against the deep indigo sky. Her world is still—just her and the rhythmic pulse of her own breath. In this solitude, she asks a question so timeless and profound it could belong to any soul in any century: *Why am I here?*

The question isn't born of despair but of yearning—a hunger to understand something larger than herself. She looks at the vast expanse of sky, stars fading as the sun prepares its debut, and she feels the weight of her smallness. And yet, within that smallness, there is a spark—a whisper that perhaps she is part of something infinite.

She doesn't know it yet, but in that quiet moment, she's tapping into a truth that has shaped civilizations, inspired revolutions, and brought solace to seekers: there is a connection, a bridge between what we see and what we sense. It's invisible yet undeniable. It's elusive, yet it beckons. And it's woven into the very fabric of her being.

## The Weight We Carry

Now consider this: how often do we ask that question—*Why am I here?*—in the

"

midst of our daily lives? More often, we are consumed by the noise. The ping of notifications, the weight of deadlines, the relentless pace of existence that insists we keep moving, keep striving, keep proving. We rush through our days, our weeks, and even our years as if racing toward some finish line we can't quite see.

And yet, in the quiet moments—those rare pauses between obligations—a different kind of ache emerges. It's not the ache of exhaustion or stress. It's deeper, quieter, like a faint knock on the door of your soul. It's the sense that, despite all the motion, something is missing. A sense of *disconnection.*

You may feel it when you scroll through social media, envying lives that look polished and purposeful. You may feel it in the monotony of routines that once seemed full of promise. You may feel it in the stillness of the night when the distractions fall away, leaving only the quiet hum of your thoughts.

Disconnection isn't always loud, but it is persistent. It seeps into your relationships, your work, and even your dreams. It convinces you that something is wrong with *you*—that you aren't doing enough, that you aren't good enough, that maybe, just maybe, this is all there is.

But here's the secret the noise doesn't want you to know: you are not broken. You are not lost. And you are not alone.

## A World That Promised More

Do you remember a time when you believed the world was full of magic? Maybe it was childhood when fireflies were fairies, the wind carried secrets, and the stars seemed to shine just for you. Back then, the world didn't need to make sense to be beautiful. It simply was.

But as we grow, the world teaches us a different lesson. It tells us to be realistic, to focus on the tangible, and to measure our worth in achievements and outcomes. It replaces wonder with practicality, mystery with certainty, and intuition with data. It's no wonder so many of us feel trapped as if we've been handed a script we never agreed to follow.

And yet, that spark of magic never truly leaves us. It flickers in the moments we can't explain: the serendipity of meeting someone at just the right time, the comfort of a dream that feels more like a message, the way music can stir emotions we didn't know we were holding. These moments remind us that there is more to life than what we can see or measure.

But how do we access that *more?* How do we move beyond the surface of life and reconnect with something deeper, something that feels like *home?*

## A Glimpse of Possibility

What if the answer isn't about *adding* anything to your life but about *removing* what doesn't belong? What if the connection you're yearning for isn't out there, but within you? What if, right now, you already have everything you need to feel whole, to feel purpose, to feel alive?

Picture this: a life where you wake up not with dread or urgency but with quiet anticipation. A life where your choices feel aligned with your deepest values, where your relationships feel meaningful, and where even the simplest moments carry a sense of wonder. It's not about perfection or avoiding hardship. It's about knowing, deep in your bones, that you are part of something infinite and extraordinary—and that your existence matters.

This isn't wishful thinking. It's not about escaping reality or denying the challenges of life. It's about discovering a way to live that honors both the tangible and the transcendent, the seen and the unseen, the finite and the infinite.

And it begins with a single question: What if there's *more?*

## The Journey Home

There's a reason you picked up this book. Maybe you can't quite put it into words, but something brought you here—a curiosity, a hope, or perhaps that faint knock on your soul's door. Whatever the reason, know this: you are not here by accident.

You are part of a story far greater than you can imagine. It's a story of creation and connection, of mystery and meaning. And though the details of your journey are uniquely yours, the essence is universal. We are all seeking the same thing: to know that we belong, to feel that our lives have purpose, and to trust that we are not alone in the vastness of existence.

As you turn the page, you will not find answers handed to you. What you will find are questions—questions that invite you to explore, to reflect, and to remember. You will find tools and insights to help you navigate the unknown, not as a map but as a compass. And most importantly, you will find an invitation to reconnect with the divine thread that weaves through all of life.

So take a deep breath. Let go of the noise, the expectations, the doubts that have weighed you down. Open your heart to the possibility that you are more connected, more powerful, and more loved than you've ever dared to believe.

*Because you are.*

## The Path Unfolds

There is a journey awaiting you, one that doesn't begin with a grand departure or a distant destination. It starts right here, in the stillness of this moment, with the quiet question that lingers in the depths of your heart: *What does it mean to truly live?*

You are about to embark on a journey that is as much inward as it is outward, one that will take you beyond the boundaries of what you thought was possible. You will explore the intersection of science and spirit, where ancient wisdom meets modern discovery, and where the seemingly ordinary reveals its extraordinary depths.

By the time we are finished, you will not simply *know* concepts—you will *feel* them. You will have the tools to align your thoughts, intentions, and actions with the unseen currents that shape our reality. You will understand the profound connection between your inner world and the infinite quantum field, and you'll discover how to live in harmony with it. This isn't a guide to temporary inspiration; it's an invitation to transformation.

## The Why Behind the Words

Before we step fully into this exploration, let me share with you why I am here, writing these words, and why this path is one I feel compelled to walk with you.

For as long as I can remember, I have been captivated by two great mysteries: the vast, intricate dance of the cosmos and the quiet, inner landscape of the soul. As a child, I would stare at the night sky, not just marveling at the stars but *feeling* them—as if they were calling to something deep within me. That sense of awe never left me. It grew into a lifelong pursuit to understand the unseen forces that connect everything, from the smallest particle to the farthest galaxy.

My professional journey has been equally diverse, spanning fields that might seem worlds apart: physics and metaphysics, philosophy and psychology, ancient traditions, and cutting-edge technology. Each path, though seemingly distinct, led me to the same realization: there is no separation between the scientific and the spiritual. They are two languages describing the same truth. And at the heart of that truth is connection—the profound, unshakable unity that binds us to one another, to the universe, and to the Creator.

But I am not here as a teacher above you; I am a fellow traveler. Like you, I have wrestled with doubt and disconnection. I have felt the pull of life's noise, the distraction of its demands. And I have learned, again and again, that the answers we seek are not *out there* but *within*. This book is not a culmination of what I know; it's a celebration of what I've discovered—and what I continue to discover every day.

## What Awaits You

Through these pages, we will explore ideas that are both timeless and timely, rooted in ancient wisdom and illuminated by modern science. You'll come to understand how your thoughts and intentions ripple through the quantum field, influencing outcomes in ways both subtle and profound. You'll learn how to align yourself with the natural rhythms of the universe, creating a life that feels not just productive but purposeful. And you'll uncover the tools to cultivate connection— not just with the divine, but with yourself, your community, and the greater whole.

Let me tell you what this is *not*. It is not a book about abstract theories or impractical ideals. Every concept we discuss is grounded in something tangible— whether it's a personal practice, a scientific principle, or a universal truth. You won't simply read about transformation; you'll experience it.

The ideas may challenge you. They may ask you to see the world—and yourself—in a new light. But isn't that why you're here? To grow, to stretch, to reach for something greater? The world doesn't need more certainty; it needs curiosity. It doesn't need more control; it needs connection. And it doesn't need more noise; it needs stillness. Together, we'll explore how to bring these qualities into your life, not as fleeting moments but as a way of being.

## The Heart of the Journey

You may be wondering what makes this path any different from the countless others promising fulfillment and purpose. The answer is simple: this journey is *yours*. It is not a prescription or a formula but a map for discovering the truth that already resides within you. The insights and practices we'll explore are not about adding something to your life; they are about uncovering what's already there, waiting to be awakened.

You will find that the concepts we explore are interconnected, much like the web of life itself. From the quantum field to the power of intention, from ancient wisdom to modern science, each thread weaves into the next, creating a tapestry of understanding that is both intricate and beautifully simple. As we delve into these ideas, you may feel moments of recognition, as if you are rediscovering something you've always known. That's because the truth is never far from us; it's just waiting for us to turn toward it.

## A Word of Encouragement

Before we begin, let me offer you this: you are ready. Whether you feel it or not, whether you know it or not, the very fact that you are here, holding these words, is a testament to your readiness. The journey ahead may ask much of you—openness, curiosity, trust—but it will give so much more in return. It will give you clarity where there is confusion, purpose where there is doubt, and connection where there is isolation.

So take a deep breath. Let this moment be the beginning of something new, something profound, something deeply personal. Let it be the moment you turn toward the infinite and say, *Yes.* Yes to the questions, yes to the mystery, yes to the life that is waiting for you.

Shall we step into the unknown, together?

# Chapter One

# The Quantum Field: A Cosmic Blueprint

*"Science is not only compatible with spirituality;
it is a profound source of spirituality."*
— Carl Sagan

Envision, if you will, an ocean—but not the kind you've ever seen before. This ocean is boundless, shimmering with light, alive with an energy that hums beneath the surface. It isn't just water; it is a tapestry of potential, a web connecting everything you've ever known. Here, in this cosmic ocean, we find the quantum field—the unseen design of the universe, where possibility becomes reality within the remarkable framework upon which all existence rests. Together, we'll uncover its mysteries, its connections that defy space and time, and the divine intelligence it mirrors.

## What Is the Quantum Field? (The Cosmic Sea of Potential)

Imagine you're sitting on the edge of a dock at sunrise. The air is still, and the water below stretches endlessly, reflecting colors that change with each passing moment. Now, imagine that every ripple in this vast ocean is part of something greater—a network, a conversation of energy and possibility. That, my friend, is the quantum field.

It's not something you can touch or see, but it's as real as the ground beneath your feet. Scientists describe it as the framework of all existence, a place where particles and waves weave the fabric of reality. Spiritually, it is the essence of creation, a divine canvas where the infinite becomes the tangible.

## The Field of Infinite Possibilities

Let's break it down. Everything—yes, everything—starts as potential. The chair you're sitting on, the stars in the night sky, even the words on this page—all began as a possibility within the quantum field. This field doesn't operate like the physical world you know; it's a realm of probabilities, not certainties. Here, nothing is fixed until it's observed.

Think of it as a game of chess. Before a move is made, countless possibilities exist. But once you move that pawn or knight, a new reality unfolds. The quantum field is the chessboard of the cosmos, and every thought, every action, is a move that shapes the game.

## The Energy Beneath the Surface

Here's where it gets fascinating. Even in the emptiest corners of the universe, there is energy. Scientists call it *zero-point energy,* a kind of background hum that's always there. This energy isn't loud or obvious, but it's the very fabric of reality—a subtle but powerful force that holds everything together.

Imagine this energy as a spider's web. It's delicate but strong, connecting every point to every other. Tug on one thread, and the entire web feels it. This is how the quantum field works: an interconnected network of energy that links every atom, thought, and being in the universe. It's here that science and spirituality shake hands.

---

**Zero-Point Energy:** Even at the coldest temperature possible, called absolute zero, tiny particles like atoms and electrons still have some energy and never completely stop moving. This remaining energy is called zero-point energy. It happens because, in the world of quantum physics, particles can't be perfectly still or precisely located due to the rules of uncertainty.

---

## Observing the Observer

Here's a question for you: Have you ever noticed how the simple act of paying attention changes things? In quantum physics, this is called the observer effect. When we focus on something, we influence its outcome. In the quantum field, observation collapses potential into reality.

Let's put it this way: When you set your sights on a goal, you're not just hoping for the best. You're actively shaping the field of possibilities. Every thought, every intention, is like dropping a pebble into that cosmic ocean, sending ripples outward. This is how we co-create our reality with the quantum field.

> **Observer Effect:** The observer effect means that just by looking at or measuring something, we can change how it behaves. In the tiny world of atoms and particles, when scientists try to watch what's happening, their tools can disturb the particles and cause different results than if they weren't being watched. It's like when someone acts differently because they know they're being watched–it's similar for particles in experiments.

## Reflective Exercise: Experiencing the Field

Take a moment—yes, right now—to close your eyes. Picture yourself standing by that infinite ocean we spoke of earlier. Feel the energy of the waves as they wash over your feet. Breathe deeply. With each inhale, sense the potential surrounding you. Now, ask yourself: What ripple am I creating? What wave am I sending out into this field of endless possibility? Pause and listen. The answer is already within you.

### Where Science Meets Spirit

For as long as we've been gazing at the stars or sitting in quiet meditation, we've been trying to understand the forces that shape our world. Ancient wisdom spoke of an interconnected essence, while modern science offers equations and experiments. But these are not opposing views; they're two sides of the same coin.

The quantum field is where these perspectives meet. It's a place of awe and wonder, a space where intellect and intuition blend seamlessly. To explore it is to step into a world of infinite potential, a reminder that we are both humble observers and active participants in the grand design.

Ahead lies the mystery of connections that defy time and space, the unfolding of reality from the wave function, and the divine order that gives it all meaning.

## Nonlocality: Mysterious Connections Across Space and Time

Let me tell you a story. In 1935, three brilliant minds—Einstein, Podolsky, and Rosen—posed a question that shook the foundations of physics. They suggested that particles, once linked, could remain connected no matter the distance. Einstein called it "spooky action at a distance." And spooky it is, but it's also real. This phenomenon is known as *nonlocality*.

Nonlocality is the idea that particles can communicate instantaneously across vast distances. Imagine twins who, though separated by thousands of miles, feel the same joy and the same sorrow at the same moment. But these twins aren't people; they're particles—tiny, subatomic messengers sending signals faster than the speed of light.

You see, nonlocality defies what we think we know about the world. How can something here instantly affect something over there? It's as if the universe itself refuses to acknowledge boundaries. This interconnectedness isn't just theoretical; it's been observed in laboratories. When one particle is measured, its twin reacts, even if they are separated by galaxies.

---

**Nonlocality:** Nonlocality is a strange idea in science that says tiny particles, like atoms, can stay connected to each other no matter how far apart they are. If one particle changes, the other one changes instantly, even if they're on opposite sides of the planet–or even the universe. This connection happens faster than the speed of light, and scientists are still trying to understand how it works.

---

## The Cosmic Implication

Now, let's think bigger. If particles can be connected across space and time, what does that mean for you and me? Could it be that our thoughts, our prayers, our intentions ripple through this same invisible thread? Nonlocality hints that we are not isolated islands but part of an interconnected web, where every action, every thought, reverberates far beyond its point of origin.

Think of it as a cosmic symphony. Each note, no matter how faint, contributes to the harmony. The vibrations of your life—your kindness, your creativity, your love—may touch someone on the other side of the world or perhaps the other side of the universe.

Nonlocality is the science that suggests we are, quite literally, never alone.

---

## Reflective Exercise: Tapping into Connection

Take a moment to consider someone you care about deeply. Please close your eyes and imagine a thread of light connecting you to them, no matter the distance. Picture your love and gratitude traveling along that thread, reaching them in an instant. What do you feel in return? Hold onto that feeling. It is a glimpse of the quantum connection that binds us all.

---

## Where Mystery Meets Meaning

Nonlocality reminds us that the universe is stranger and more wondrous than we can imagine. It's a concept that leaves scientists scratching their heads and mystics nodding knowingly. It suggests that the barriers we see—time, space, separation—are illusions. And in their place, we find something extraordinary: unity.

# Wave Function: The Nature of Potential and Reality

To understand how the quantum field moves from possibility to reality, we must journey deeper into the heart of quantum mechanics. Enter the *wave function*, a mathematical description of the probabilities that exist within the field. Think of it as a map—not of roads or rivers, but of potential paths reality might take.

The wave function is like a symphony, each note representing a possibility. Before the music plays, all the notes exist at once, coiled tightly in a state of readiness. This is called superposition. But when the first note is struck, the symphony begins, and one reality emerges from the quantum sea.

> **Wave Function:** A wave function is a math tool that helps scientists describe and predict what tiny particles, like electrons, might do. Instead of saying exactly where a particle is or how fast it's moving, the wave function shows all the possible places the particle could be at once. When someone measures the particle, the wave function "collapses," and the particle chooses one spot or state.

## The Collapse of Possibility

Imagine rolling a pair of dice. Before they land, every number between two and twelve is possible. But the moment they stop, a single outcome becomes real. This is how the wave function collapses, turning potential into reality. But here's the twist: in the quantum world, it's our observation that rolls the dice.

Our thoughts and actions act like a conductor, calling forth the notes of the symphony. When you focus your energy—whether on a goal, a prayer, or even a moment of gratitude—you collapse the wave function, pulling a specific possibility into existence.

In this way, the quantum field responds to the intentions we set.

## Reflective Exercise: Shaping Reality

Close your eyes. Picture a moment in your life where you felt deep gratitude or joy. Hold onto that feeling, letting it expand within you. Now, imagine sending that energy into the quantum field as though you're planting a seed in fertile soil. What do you wish to grow? Take a deep breath, and know that the seed has been sown.

### The Mystery of Superposition

While the wave function brings reality into focus, it also reminds us of the vastness of potential. In *superposition*, all possibilities exist simultaneously. It's like standing at a crossroads with infinite paths before you, each one a different outcome of your choices and intentions.

The beauty of this mystery is its power to inspire. It suggests that no matter where you are or what challenges you face, there is always another possibility waiting. Reality is not fixed; it is fluid, shaped by your thoughts, your actions, and your faith in what could be.

> **Superposition** refers to the ability of a particle to exist in multiple states or locations simultaneously until it is observed or measured, at which point it collapses into a single state.

### Where Potential Becomes Power

The wave function teaches us that potential is not passive. It is alive, humming with energy, ready to respond to our intentions. It invites us to see ourselves not as bystanders but as co-creators in the unfolding story of the universe.

And so, as we move forward, we'll explore the principles that guide this cosmic dance, from the Logos that orders the universe to the holographic nature that reflects its unity.

## Introducing Logos: The Principle of Universal Order

And now, let's consider the word "*Logos*." Not just a word but a principle—one that has shaped philosophies, religions, and even the foundations of science. In ancient Greek thought, Logos meant reason, order, or a governing principle. To the philosophers of old, it was the thread that wove the cosmos into harmony.

> **Logos**: In ancient Greek philosophy, Logos refers to the principle of reason, order, and logic governing the universe. It has also been used in Christian theology to denote the divine Word or creative force, emphasizing its connection to universal intelligence and creation.

However, Logos is not just a relic of intellectual history. It is alive and well within the quantum field, the very force that whispers to the particles, guiding their dance and aligning their chaos into creation. Imagine, if you will, a conductor standing before an orchestra. Without guidance, the musicians might play at random. But with the sweep of a baton, chaos transforms into a symphony. That baton, that guiding force, is the Logos.

## The Language of the Universe

Think for a moment about the beauty of nature. A snowflake's intricate design, the spirals of a sunflower, the galaxies spinning in the heavens—all speak a language of order. This is the Logos at work. In the quantum field, it acts as a blueprint, a divine script that informs the unfolding of reality.

Just as an architect lays out plans for a building, the Logos maps the structure of the universe. But unlike human blueprints, this one is alive, adapting and responding to the intentions of those who engage with it. It is, in a sense, the cosmic law that ensures the universe doesn't unravel into chaos.

---

## Reflective Exercise: Connecting with Logos

Close your eyes and think of a moment in your life that felt serendipitous, as if everything fell perfectly into place. Now, imagine that moment as a thread woven into the fabric of existence, a part of the greater design. Breathe deeply and ask yourself: How can I align my actions with the order of the universe? What small step can I take today to honor the harmony that surrounds me?

---

## Where Order Meets Intention

What makes Logos truly remarkable is its relationship with intention. While it provides the structure, it does not dictate the outcome. Instead, it partners with consciousness, responding to the energy we bring into the field. This is why prayer, meditation, and focused thought hold such power—they align us with the Logos, tuning our frequency to the divine order of the cosmos.

It is said that when we act in harmony with the Logos, life flows with an ease that feels almost magical. Obstacles seem to dissolve, and opportunities appear as if by design. But this is no magic trick; it is the universe responding to our alignment with its laws.

### A Principle of Unity

Ultimately, the Logos reminds us that we are not separate from the universe—we are part of its design. It calls us to step into our role as co-creators, to live with purpose and intention, and to trust in the order that holds all things together. And as we embrace this principle, we find not only connection but also profound peace.

Ahead lies the exploration of how this design reflects in every fragment of existence—the *holographic nature* of the universe itself.

## The Holographic Universe: Every Part Reflects the Whole

Now, picture holding a small, intricate glass sphere in your hand. Inside, the entire night sky is reflected—each star, each constellation, shimmering as though alive. But here's the marvel: if you were to break that sphere into a thousand pieces, each fragment would still contain the image of the entire sky. That, my friend, is the essence of the holographic universe.

The holographic principle suggests that every part of the universe contains the blueprint of the whole. In other words, you are not just part of the universe—you are a microcosm of it. The quantum field, the Logos, the entire cosmic design—it all exists within you, as much as you exist within it.

> **Holographic Universe** theory suggests that the three-dimensional reality we experience may be encoded on a two-dimensional surface, much like a hologram. This concept, rooted in quantum physics and string theory, proposes that all the information of the universe is interconnected and stored in a unified field.

### The Science Behind the Metaphor

The holographic nature of the universe is not merely poetic. Physicists have found evidence suggesting that the fabric of reality operates like a hologram. Information about the entirety of the cosmos can be encoded in even the smallest fragment. This means that the vast complexity of the universe is not stored "out there" but within every particle, every atom, every being.

### What It Means for Us

If the universe is holographic, then the connection between all things is not just a philosophical idea—it's a scientific reality. This principle reinforces the idea of unity, of oneness. It tells us that the Divine is not something distant and separate but intimately woven into the very fabric of our being.

Think of your own body. Every cell contains the complete DNA blueprint that makes you who you are. Similarly, every soul, every spark of consciousness, carries within it the fingerprint of the cosmos. When you gaze at the stars, you are, in a way, looking at yourself.

## Reflective Exercise: Seeing the Whole Within the Part

Close your eyes and bring to mind something small and simple—a leaf, a grain of sand, a drop of water. Imagine it glowing with life, containing within it the entire story of existence. Now, turn inward. Visualize that same glow within your heart, your mind, and your soul. Breathe deeply and sense the infinite within you. What does it reveal?

### The Universe Within

The holographic principle invites you to see the world—and yourself—with new eyes. It encourages us to find the whole within the part and to recognize that even the smallest actions and thoughts can echo through the cosmos. When we embrace this truth, we begin to live with greater awareness, knowing that the entirety of creation resides within us.

And so, we return to the idea of the quantum field, this vast ocean of potential. But now, we see it not just as something external but as something deeply personal. You are not merely in the universe—the universe is in you.

## Revisiting the Core Concepts and Insights

The **quantum field** is not just a concept confined to the world of physics; it is the very fabric of existence, a dynamic and infinite sea of possibilities that stretches beyond what our senses can perceive. Everything we've explored in this chapter points to a profound truth: the universe is alive, interconnected, and deeply responsive to consciousness.

Think about the concept of **nonlocality**—the idea that particles can remain connected across vast distances. It challenges the very boundaries of what we consider possible, revealing that separation is an illusion. This isn't just about particles; it's about us, our relationships, our intentions. In a universe where everything is connected, every thought and every action sends ripples through the cosmic web.

The **wave function**, that elegant mathematical construct, teaches us that potential is a living force waiting for our intention to shape it. It reminds us that we are not passive observers but active participants in the unfolding of reality. Each choice we make, each thought we hold, collapses possibility into form, bringing the abstract into the tangible.

Then there is **Logos**—the principle of universal order, the guiding intelligence that orchestrates the dance of creation. The Logos speaks to the inherent harmony of the universe, a harmony that we can tune into through our own alignment with intention and purpose. It is both a cosmic law and a personal guide, a reminder that we are deeply connected to the greater design.

Finally, the **holographic nature** of the universe ties it all together. It shows us that the whole is reflected in every part and that we carry within us the blueprint of the cosmos. This is not a metaphor—it is a reality supported by science and echoed by spirituality. When we begin to see the universe within ourselves, we understand our true power and potential.

The quantum field, the wave function, the Logos, and the holographic principle are not separate ideas. They are threads in a single tapestry, each contributing to a picture of a universe that is alive, interconnected, and full of possibility. They invite us to live with greater awareness, to see ourselves not as small and insignificant but as co-creators in a grand cosmic symphony.

...

And so, we have set the stage. We've explored the quantum field as the blueprint of existence, but there's more to this story. What role do we, as conscious beings, play in this grand design? How do our thoughts, our emotions, and our very awareness interact with this vast ocean of potential? These questions lead us deeper into the mystery, where science meets spirit and where the true power of consciousness begins to emerge.

The next step in our journey awaits, and it promises to reveal how the universe does not just shape us, but we are shaping it with every breath, every thought, every intention.

# Chapter Two

# Consciousness as the Key to the Quantum Field

*"I regard consciousness as fundamental. I regard matter as derivative from consciousness."*

– Max Planck

What if I told you that the most powerful tool for shaping reality isn't found in laboratories or cathedrals but within you? Imagine for a moment that your thoughts, your focus, and your emotions are not confined to the boundaries of your mind but ripple through the very fabric of existence. This is the profound connection between consciousness and the quantum field—a relationship that bridges the gap between science and spirituality.

By understanding how consciousness interacts with this boundless matrix of potential, we uncover the astonishing ways in which attention and intention shape the world around us. From the observer effect in quantum physics to the energetic resonance of our thoughts and emotions, we will see that consciousness is not just a participant in the universe but a co-creator.

## The Observer Effect: How Attention Collapses Potential into Reality

Imagine standing in a room filled with countless doors, each leading to a different path, a different outcome. The doors remain closed until you choose one. The moment your hand touches a handle, that door opens, and the *infinite possibilities* collapse into a single reality. This, in essence, is the observer effect—a phenomenon in quantum physics that demonstrates how observation influences outcomes.

## The Science Behind Observation

The observer effect is one of the most fascinating discoveries in quantum mechanics. It shows that particles exist in a state of superposition—a condition where all possibilities coexist simultaneously—until they are observed. When measured, these particles choose a specific state, collapsing the wave of potential into a concrete reality.

But what does this mean for you? To grasp the significance, consider that your attention acts like the observer in these experiments. Where you direct your focus, you influence outcomes. It's as though your consciousness carries the power to shape reality itself.

## Consciousness as a Creative Force

Pause for a moment and reflect: How often do we act as passive spectators in our own lives, believing that external forces dictate our circumstances? The observer effect suggests a far more empowering truth. Your attention—your conscious awareness—is an active participant in the unfolding of your reality.

Think of your thoughts as a flashlight in a dark room. Whatever you shine the beam on becomes illuminated, brought into your awareness. The quantum field, like that room, holds infinite possibilities. By focusing your attention, you light up a specific path, collapsing the wave of potential and bringing it into existence.

---

### Reflective Exercise: Where Is Your Attention?

Take a moment to sit quietly. Close your eyes and imagine a blank canvas stretched out before you. What do you want to paint on this canvas? A goal? A dream? A resolution? Picture it clearly. Now ask yourself: Where am I directing my attention in daily life? Does it align with the image I'm creating? Breathe deeply, and visualize your focus sharpening, illuminating the path toward your chosen reality.

---

Have you ever noticed how focusing intently on something—a project, a relationship, a challenge—seems to draw events and opportunities aligned with that focus? It's no coincidence. Whether you're aware of it or not, your consciousness acts as a magnet, attracting experiences that resonate with your mental and emotional energy.

## | *Stories from Everyday Life* |

Have you ever heard of **Jim Carrey's** now-famous story about his $10 million check? In the early 1990s, before his meteoric rise to fame, Carrey wrote himself a check for $10 million for "acting services rendered," post-dated it for five years in the future, and carried it in his wallet. Every day, he visualized himself achieving his goal, imagining the life he wanted as if it had already come to pass. Within that timeframe, he landed his breakout roles in *Ace Ventura: Pet Detective* and *The Mask*, earning exactly the amount he had envisioned.

Or take **Oprah Winfrey's** belief in the power of intention. In her career, Oprah has spoken extensively about visualizing success before it materialized. In her early days, she imagined herself interviewing powerful figures and connecting deeply with audiences worldwide. This mental focus not only shaped her career but also drew opportunities that aligned with her aspirations. From producing her own network to becoming a global figure in philanthropy and empowerment, her life reflects the profound influence of focused intention.

Then there's **J.K. Rowling,** who envisioned her book series becoming a global phenomenon long before Harry Potter became a household name. Despite being rejected by 12 publishers, Rowling held onto her vision. She would sit in cafes, imagining her books in the hands of readers everywhere, letting her creative process fuel her belief. Today, Harry Potter is one of the most successful book franchises in history.

---

These real-life examples illustrate the principle behind focused consciousness. When you align your thoughts and emotions with a vision, you amplify your energy and create a resonance that draws people, events, and opportunities into your life. Like the observer in quantum physics collapsing waves of possibility, your awareness helps shape reality. Whether it's visualizing success, writing a check to your future self, or persevering against rejection, focused intention becomes the key to unlocking the potential waiting in the quantum field.

### The Spiritual Implications

The observer effect not only bridges science and spirituality but invites us to see the sacred role of our consciousness. In the context of the divine, your ability to focus is a gift—a way to co-create with the Creator. Each thought, each moment of attention, becomes a prayer sent into the quantum field, aligning with the potential waiting to unfold.

### Practical Insights for Daily Living

So, how can you harness the power of your attention to shape your life? Begin with awareness. Notice where your thoughts dwell throughout the day. Are you focusing on possibilities or limitations? Joy or fear? Remember, the quantum field responds to your consciousness, amplifying what you give your energy to. By practicing mindfulness and intention, you can direct this incredible creative force toward outcomes that align with your highest purpose.

And here lies the beauty: The observer effect is not bound by physical proximity or time. Whether you are meditating on a distant goal or offering a silent prayer, your focused consciousness interacts with the quantum field, sending ripples across the fabric of existence. It is here, in this interplay of thought and reality, that the bridge between science and spirituality becomes most evident.

## The Mind–Field Connection: Bridging Thought and the Quantum Field

Now, imagine your mind as an antenna, constantly sending and receiving signals across the vast ocean of the quantum field. Each thought you have, each intention you hold, is like a broadcast, rippling outward into this infinite expanse. But here's the wonder: the quantum field isn't just a passive receiver. It responds, rearranging itself to reflect the vibrations you send.

### Thoughts as Energy

Let's start with a simple truth: thoughts are not intangible whispers confined to the mind. They are forms of energy that are measurable and real. Neuroscientists have discovered that every thought creates electrical impulses in the brain, while spiritual traditions have long taught that thoughts carry vibrational frequencies. In the context of the quantum field, these frequencies act as instructions, shaping the probabilities that surround us.

Think of a radio station. If you want to hear classical music, you must tune in to the right frequency. Your mind works the same way. When you focus your thoughts on love, gratitude, or abundance, you align your frequency with those possibilities in the quantum field. Conversely, thoughts of fear or lack can tune you to experiences that reflect those vibrations.

> **Mind-Field Connection:** The mind-field connection is the idea that our thoughts and intentions can interact with an invisible energy field that connects everything in the universe. This field, the "quantum field," holds endless possibilities, and our minds can influence these possibilities to shape what happens in our lives.

## The Power of Intent

Intent is thought with direction and purpose. While fleeting thoughts may ripple faintly through the quantum field, focused intent sends a powerful wave. It's like tossing a stone into a pond. A small pebble creates ripples, but a larger stone sends waves that reach the farthest edges.

Throughout history, individuals have harnessed the power of intent to create profound change. Consider the practice of prayer, where intention meets faith, or meditation, where focused thought aligns with inner stillness. These practices are not merely acts of tradition; they are mechanisms for bridging the mind and the quantum field.

## Reflective Exercise: Tuning Your Mind

Take a moment now. Close your eyes and imagine yourself as that antenna, broadcasting your thoughts into the quantum field. What are you transmitting? Is it clarity or confusion? Hope or doubt? Picture yourself adjusting the dial and fine-tuning your thoughts to align with your highest aspirations. Feel the shift in energy as you tune in to a frequency of possibility and purpose.

## A Two-Way Connection

The connection between the mind and the quantum field is not one-sided. Just as you broadcast thoughts into the field, you also receive insights, inspirations, and synchronicities in return. Have you ever had a sudden idea or encountered a coincidence that seemed too perfect to ignore? These moments are the quantum field responding to your vibrational output, offering guidance and aligning opportunities.

One story that comes to mind is that of a teacher who longed to help underserved communities. She spent hours each day visualizing the impact she wanted to make, imagining the faces of the children she hoped to teach. One day, seemingly out of nowhere, she was introduced to someone who shared her vision and provided the resources to start a nonprofit organization.

Or take the story of Dr. James R. Doty, a clinical professor of neurosurgery at Stanford University, who grew up in poverty with an alcoholic father and a mother who battled depression. At the age of 12, he wandered into a magic shop, where he met Ruth, the owner's mother. Recognizing his difficult circumstances, Ruth taught him techniques involving mindfulness, visualization, and setting clear intentions.

These practices enabled Doty to envision a different future for himself, fostering a sense of purpose and direction. Was it coincidence? Or was it the quantum field responding to the energy of his focused intent?

### The Divine Dialogue

The mind-field connection reveals something deeply sacred: we are in constant dialogue with creation itself. Every thought, every intention, becomes a thread woven into the tapestry of existence. The quantum field listens, not with ears but with energy, and it speaks back in the language of *synchronicity,* intuition, and unfolding possibilities.

By recognizing this connection, we step into our role as active participants in the divine design. We see that our thoughts are not trivial; they are profound acts of creation, each one echoing through the vast expanse of the universe. In this understanding, we find both power and responsibility—the power to shape reality and the responsibility to align our thoughts with love, purpose, and the greater good.

---

**Synchronicity:** Just as two entangled particles influence each other instantaneously (nonlocality and quantum entanglement), synchronicity suggests a similar interconnectedness between events, thoughts, and experiences. When two or more unrelated events align in a way that holds personal or symbolic significance for an individual, creating a sense of connection between the external world and internal experience.

---

# Energetic Contagion: How Emotions Ripple Through the Field

Now, let's shift our focus from thoughts to emotions, those unseen currents that flow through us all. Imagine standing at the edge of a still pond, tossing in a stone. The ripples spread outward, touching everything in their path. In much the same way, your emotions ripple through the quantum field, influencing not only your own reality but the realities of those around you.

## The Energy of Emotion

Emotions, like thoughts, carry a vibrational frequency. Joy, love, and gratitude resonate at higher frequencies, while fear, anger, and despair vibrate at lower ones. These frequencies act as signals, broadcasting your inner state to the quantum field. But emotions are more than signals—they are also amplifiers. A thought infused with emotion carries far more energy than a thought alone.

*Picture this:* A heartfelt prayer, spoken with tears of hope, carries a different weight than a mechanical recitation. Why? Because emotion energizes intention. It transforms a simple ripple into a wave that moves the quantum field more powerfully.

## The Ripple Effect

Now, consider how emotions extend beyond the self. Have you ever walked into a room and instantly felt the mood—whether it was joyful, tense, or somber? That's *emotional contagion* at work. Emotions are not confined to the individual; they spread, influencing the energetic atmosphere of a space and the people within it.

This phenomenon has been observed in groups of people, from families to entire communities. Positive emotions, like shared laughter or collective gratitude, create a resonance that uplifts everyone involved. Conversely, negativity can spiral, pulling others into its orbit. In this way, your emotional state becomes a contribution to the collective field.

---

### Reflective Exercise: Observing Your Emotional Ripples

Take a moment to pause and reflect on your emotional state. Close your eyes and imagine your emotions as waves radiating outward from your heart. What kind of ripples are you sending into the world? Are they waves of love and kindness, or do they carry frustration and doubt?

As you breathe deeply, visualize your emotions calming and harmonizing, transforming into ripples of compassion and peace that touch everything in their path. Feel the warmth of this shift and recognize the power you hold to influence the quantum field with your inner state.

---

## | *Stories of Emotional Resonance* |

The impact of emotional contagion can be vividly seen in real-life events, from personal interactions to global movements. One powerful example comes from the aftermath of Hurricane Harvey in 2017, which devastated communities in Texas. Amid the chaos and destruction, Houston resident **Jim McIngvale**, better known as "Mattress Mack," opened his furniture stores to serve as shelters for displaced residents. His calm demeanor, unwavering optimism, and acts of generosity created a ripple effect, inspiring other local businesses and individuals to step forward with their own acts of kindness. What began as one man's decision to help his neighbors turned into a community-wide effort that brought hope and resilience to thousands.

On a more personal level, consider the story of **Fred Rogers**—better known as "Mister Rogers." Throughout his television career, his quiet, compassionate demeanor offered reassurance and confidence to countless children. Parents have often shared how his calm and empathetic approach soothed their children's fears, whether about visiting the doctor or dealing with a bully. His emotional steadiness acted as a tuning fork, aligning the emotional state of his young viewers with feelings of safety, love, and acceptance. The effects of his presence rippled far beyond individual families, shaping generations with his unique ability to model kindness and emotional balance.

---

These examples highlight how emotions—whether courage, kindness, or love—can ripple outward, influencing the collective emotional field. Whether it's a community uniting after a disaster, a parent soothing a frightened child, or a leader sparking global change, the emotional energy of one individual has the power to shape the experiences of many. It's a testament to the interconnected nature of our realities and the profound responsibility we hold in cultivating emotions that uplift and inspire.

## The Quantum Implication

From a quantum perspective, emotional contagion reveals the fluidity of the field and its responsiveness to vibrational input. The field does not merely reflect our emotions; it amplifies them, creating patterns and possibilities that align with the energy we project. This is why cultivating positive emotional states—gratitude, love, compassion—is not just a personal practice but a universal act.

When we align our emotions with higher frequencies, we contribute to the creation of realities that reflect those vibrations. Conversely, unchecked negativity can perpetuate cycles of discord, both within and around us. The choice, as always, lies within our awareness and intention.

## Emotional Mastery: A Sacred Responsibility

The power of emotional contagion calls us to greater responsibility. To recognize that our emotions ripple outward is to acknowledge our role as co-creators within the quantum field. This does not mean suppressing negative emotions; rather, it invites us to process and transform them, allowing their energy to move through us in constructive ways.

***Consider this practice:*** When you feel overwhelmed by anger or sadness, pause and breathe. Instead of resisting the emotion, acknowledge it and ask, "What is this feeling teaching me?" In doing so, you shift from reacting to responding, from being consumed by the emotion to guiding its energy with purpose.

---

## Reflective Exercise: Harmonizing Your Emotional Field

Close your eyes and place your hand over your heart. Take a slow, deep breath, and as you exhale, imagine releasing any tension or negativity. With each inhale, picture yourself drawing in light and warmth, filling your emotional field with calm and gratitude. Visualize this light expanding outward, touching those around you with its warmth. As you open your eyes, carry this awareness into your interactions, knowing that your emotional ripples shape the collective field.

---

## A Unified Energy

Emotional contagion reminds us of the profound interconnectedness of all beings. Your joy can lift another's spirit; your love can inspire someone miles away. In the quantum field, there are no boundaries, no separations—only the constant exchange of energy that binds us all. By mastering our emotions and aligning them with higher frequencies, we not only transform our own lives but contribute to a wave of positive energy that flows through the entire field.

This understanding leads us naturally to the next step in our journey: *resonance* and *alignment*. How do we fine-tune our energetic frequencies to harmonize with the quantum field and its boundless potential? That, my friend, is where the symphony truly begins.

## Resonance and Energetic Alignment: Achieving Harmony with the Field

Imagine a violinist tuning their instrument before a performance. With each adjustment, the strings align more perfectly with the intended pitch, creating a resonance that fills the concert hall with harmony. Now, think of yourself as that violinist, and the quantum field as the symphony. To play your part beautifully, you must tune your energetic frequency to align with the field's infinite potential.

### The Principle of Resonance

Resonance occurs when two frequencies vibrate in harmony, amplifying each other's energy. In physics, this is why a singer can shatter a glass by matching its natural frequency. In the quantum field, resonance is how we synchronize our energy with desired outcomes, creating a powerful connection between intention and manifestation.

> **Resonance:** In physics, resonance refers to the phenomenon where one vibrating system influences another to oscillate at the same frequency. This occurs when the natural frequency of one object matches that of another, creating a powerful amplification of energy.

To achieve resonance with the quantum field, we must first understand the vibrational frequencies of our thoughts, emotions, and actions. Higher frequencies—those associated with love, gratitude, and purpose—create harmony with the field, while lower frequencies can create dissonance, blocking the flow of potential.

### Tuning Your Frequency

Think of your daily habits and choices as the notes you play in life's symphony. Are they in tune with the reality you wish to create? For example, practicing gratitude is like striking a perfect chord, sending waves of resonance into the quantum field. On the other hand, dwelling on fear or resentment can create discord, diminishing your connection to the field's potential.

One practical way to tune your frequency is through mindfulness and intentional living. When you wake up each morning, take a moment to set your intention for the day. Visualize yourself moving through the world with purpose and positivity, aligning your energy with the outcomes you desire.

## Reflective Exercise: Tuning Into Harmony

Close your eyes and imagine yourself as an instrument vibrating with energy. What tune are you playing? Is it one of joy and connection or one of worry and resistance? Now, picture adjusting your strings and fine-tuning your frequency until you feel a sense of harmony within. Breathe deeply, and as you exhale, imagine your energy merging with the vast symphony of the quantum field.

## The Role of Meditation and Visualization

Meditation and visualization are powerful tools for achieving energetic alignment. In meditation, we quiet the noise of the mind, allowing our frequency to stabilize and rise. Visualization adds direction to this energy, creating a clear picture of the reality we wish to resonate with.

For instance, if you are seeking greater abundance, visualize yourself already living in that state. See the details—the joy, the freedom, the opportunities. Feel the emotions associated with this reality, and allow them to amplify your vibration. This process aligns your energy with the frequency of abundance, strengthening your resonance with the quantum field.

## | *Stories of Resonance in Action* |

The power of resonance comes to life in the story of **Andrea Bocelli**, the world-renowned tenor. Born with a congenital eye condition, Bocelli lost his sight completely by the age of 12 following a football accident. Despite this immense challenge, he held fast to a vision of performing on the world's grandest stages. Each day, he devoted himself not only to honing his vocal talent but also to cultivating an unshakable belief in his purpose. Bocelli often spoke of feeling a deep spiritual connection through his music, aligning his emotions and intentions with his dreams. Over time, his unwavering resonance with this vision drew remarkable opportunities, including his pivotal meeting with Luciano Pavarotti, who would become a mentor. Today, Bocelli's performances touch millions, a testament to how tuning one's energy to a higher purpose can shape reality.

Another compelling example is the story of tennis legend **Novak Djokovic**. Early in his career, Djokovic visualized himself lifting trophies on the world's greatest courts. But his path was not without obstacles—his physical fitness, dietary struggles, and injuries threatened to derail his dreams. Refusing to give in, Djokovic embraced a holistic approach, aligning his mind and body with his goals. Through visualization, meditation, and unwavering intent, he tuned his energy to match his aspirations. Today, Djokovic is one of the most decorated athletes in tennis history, a testament to how resonance amplifies intention.

---

These stories illustrate the profound impact of aligning one's energy with a vision. Like the musician in the original tale, Bocelli, Oprah, and Djokovic each tuned their frequencies through focus, practice, and unwavering belief, allowing the quantum field to align opportunities in their favor. Resonance, as these examples show, transforms potential into reality when paired with purpose and action.

## Aligning with the Divine

Resonance is not merely about achieving personal goals; it is a way of aligning with the divine flow of the universe. When we harmonize our energy with love, compassion, and gratitude, we participate in the greater symphony of creation. This alignment brings a sense of peace and purpose, reminding us that we are co-creators in a universe rich with potential.

---

### Reflective Exercise: Becoming One with the Symphony

As you close this section, take a moment to reflect on your place in the universal symphony. Close your eyes and imagine the quantum field as an infinite orchestra, each instrument playing its unique part. Now, see yourself joining in, your energy blending seamlessly with the whole. Feel the harmony, the connection, and the boundless potential that comes from being in tune with the field. Carry this awareness with you, and let it guide your actions, your intentions, and your dreams.

---

## Revisiting the Core Concepts and Insights

As we step back and look at the journey through this chapter, a profound realization emerges: consciousness is not merely a witness to the unfolding universe; it is an active participant, shaping reality through its focus, intent, and resonance. The interplay between your thoughts, emotions, and the quantum field reveals a sacred partnership—one where the individual and the cosmos co-create the symphony of existence.

The **observer effect** reminds us that where we direct our attention, we influence outcomes. In the quantum field, potential becomes reality not by chance but by the deliberate act of observation. Your awareness is the brush that paints the canvas of possibility.

The **mind-field connection** expands this idea, showing us that our thoughts are not contained within the boundaries of the mind but ripple outward, weaving into the fabric of the quantum field. Each thought, when infused with intent, becomes a powerful wave that shapes the probabilities of the universe.

Then comes the profound **impact of emotions.** More than fleeting experiences, they are energetic signatures that amplify the vibrational message of our thoughts. Love, gratitude, and compassion elevate this frequency, creating ripples that harmonize with the highest potentials of the field.

Finally, **resonance** and **energetic alignment** bring it all together. By tuning our frequencies through mindfulness, meditation, and intentional living, we align ourselves with the divine flow of the universe. This alignment not only transforms our personal realities but also contributes to collective harmony, reminding us that we are part of something infinitely greater than ourselves.

These insights are not theoretical concepts; they are calls to action. They invite us to live with greater awareness, to choose our thoughts and emotions wisely, and to embrace the divine partnership offered by the quantum field. In doing so, we discover our profound ability to create, connect, and contribute to the universal symphony.

...

As we reflect on the symphony of the quantum field, the next question arises: how do these principles play out on a cosmic scale? What does it mean to live in harmony with the universe's rhythms? Ahead, we will explore the interconnectedness of all existence, diving deeper into the resonance that unites us with the cosmos.

Stay with me—there is a melody waiting to be uncovered.

# Chapter Three

# The Symphony of the Universe: Resonance and Coherence

*"Happiness is when what you think, what you say,
and what you do are in harmony."*

– Mahatma Gandhi

Imagine standing in a vast concert hall. The room is silent yet brimming with anticipation. One by one, the musicians take their places, each tuning their instruments. At first, the sounds are scattered and chaotic, a jumble of frequencies searching for alignment. But then, the conductor lifts their baton, and in an instant, the disparate sounds transform into a harmonious symphony. Each note complements the next, creating music so powerful it seems to connect the audience to something greater than themselves. Now, imagine this harmony on a cosmic scale—a symphony where every particle, every thought, and every being contributes to a universal melody. This is the interconnected resonance of the universe.

In this chapter, we explore how the universe operates like a symphony, where coherence, resonance, and alignment create a profound harmony. Through the lens of quantum physics, spirituality, and ancient wisdom, we will uncover how our lives are part of this grand orchestra. By aligning with the principles of resonance, we can tune ourselves to the frequencies of connection, creativity, and divine purpose.

## Quantum Coherence: Unified States in Quantum Systems

Imagine droplets of water merging into a single wave, each moving in perfect unison, guided by an unseen rhythm that mirrors the divine harmony of creation.

Each droplet aligns not just with the wave but with a greater cosmic symphony, a testament to the power of coherence in connecting us to the sacred vibrations of the quantum field. This is *quantum coherence*—a phenomenon where particles, once seemingly independent, synchronize their states to act as one. In the world of quantum mechanics, coherence demonstrates the power of alignment on the smallest scales of existence. And yet, it holds lessons far beyond the subatomic realm, offering insights into how we, too, can align with the greater rhythm of the universe.

## The Science of Quantum Coherence

In classical physics, objects exist independently, each following its own path. But in the quantum field, particles behave differently. When particles achieve coherence, their individual states blend into a unified whole. This coherence allows them to function as a single system, amplifying their collective energy and potential. It's as if they've found a common purpose, moving together in perfect synchronization.

Consider how lasers work. Unlike ordinary light, which scatters in all directions, the light in a laser beam is coherent. The photons align their frequencies and phases, creating a focused and powerful beam capable of cutting through steel or performing delicate surgeries. This alignment is the essence of quantum coherence—small parts working in harmony to achieve extraordinary results.

> **Quantum Coherence** is a principle in quantum mechanics that describes how particles, such as electrons or photons, can exist in a harmonious, unified state, maintaining a precise relationship with each other across space and time.

## Coherence in Life

Consider the scattered notes of a symphony before the conductor's baton rises—chaotic, disconnected, yet full of potential. Now reflect on your own life. How often do your thoughts, emotions, and actions feel out of sync, like instruments playing to different rhythms? This misalignment, like scattered light, dilutes your energy and diminishes your capacity to create. However, when thoughts, emotions, and intentions move as one, you enter a state of coherence, amplifying your focus and potential like a laser beam cutting through the fog.

Take, for example, the phenomenon athletes describe as being "in the zone." This transcendent state emerges when mind, body, and spirit operate in perfect unison, enabling feats that seem almost beyond human capability. Olympic swimmer Katie Ledecky, for instance, has spoken of losing herself in the rhythm of the water, where every stroke feels effortless yet powerful—a vivid example of coherence in action, where alignment fosters extraordinary outcomes. This alignment is not coincidental—it is coherence in action, where every aspect of their being resonates with a singular purpose.

## Reflective Exercise: Finding Your Coherence

Take a moment to sit quietly. Close your eyes and picture the scattered pieces of your day—the unfinished tasks, the nagging doubts, the competing desires. Now, imagine gathering these pieces like musicians tuning their instruments. Visualize each thought and feeling, finding its place in the symphony of your life. As you breathe deeply, feel a sense of alignment and clarity emerging. In this moment of coherence, ask yourself: What is my purpose today?

## The Spiritual Implications

Coherence is not just a physical phenomenon; it acts as a dynamic connection between human intention and divine energy. This profound alignment transforms individual moments of clarity into shared waves of resonance, bridging the gap between the seen and unseen. When we align with our inner truth, we create resonance with the divine order of the universe. This alignment allows us to access deeper intuition, creativity, and connection. It is in these moments of coherence that we feel most alive, most connected to something greater than ourselves.

## Lessons from Nature

Nature offers countless examples of coherence. Consider the murmuration of starlings—hundreds of birds moving as one, creating breathtaking patterns in the sky. Scientists have marveled at how these flocks maintain such perfect synchronization with no apparent leader or plan. Yet, each bird's movements influence the whole, creating a dance that is both spontaneous and unified. This is coherence in its purest form, reminding us that alignment is not about control but about connection.

## Coherence and the Quantum Field

On the quantum level, coherence unlocks extraordinary potential. When particles achieve coherence, they exhibit phenomena such as *superconductivity* and *quantum entanglement*, where information and energy transfer instantaneously across vast distances. These principles hint at the interconnected nature of the universe, where coherence allows for instantaneous communication and limitless possibilities.

> **Superconductivity** refers to a physical phenomenon observed in certain materials at extremely low temperatures, where they exhibit zero electrical resistance and the expulsion of magnetic fields (known as the Meissner effect). Superconductors allow electric currents to flow indefinitely without energy loss.

In our own lives, coherence with the quantum field means aligning our thoughts, emotions, and intentions with the vibrations of love, gratitude, and purpose. This alignment amplifies our ability to manifest and connect, turning the chaos of potential into a symphony of creation.

## Reflective Exercise: Becoming One with the Field

Close your eyes and imagine yourself as a particle in the quantum field. Feel the scattered energy around you begin to align, each vibration finding its place in the greater whole. As you breathe deeply, sense your connection to the field growing stronger. Visualize yourself moving in harmony with the universe, each thought and intention resonating with clarity and purpose.

This state of coherence is where creation begins, where the scattered becomes unified, and where the individual becomes part of the universal symphony. It is here, in this alignment, that we discover the true power of resonance.

> **Quantum Entanglement** is a phenomenon in quantum physics where two or more particles become interconnected such that the state of one particle instantaneously influences the state of the other(s), regardless of the distance separating them.

## Resonance: Amplifying Intention Through Alignment

Now imagine striking a tuning fork and holding it near another. If both are tuned to the same frequency, the second fork begins to vibrate on its own, amplifying the sound. This phenomenon, known as resonance, demonstrates how aligned frequencies strengthen one another, creating waves of energy that ripple far beyond their origin. In the quantum field, resonance is the force that magnifies intention, transforming individual efforts into collective harmony.

## Resonance in Action

Resonance is more than a physical principle; it is a universal truth. When we align our intentions with the vibrations of the quantum field, we amplify our ability to manifest and connect. Consider a singer who shatters glass with their voice. This is not a matter of volume but of precision—their voice matches the glass's natural frequency, creating resonance so powerful it breaks the material. Similarly, when your thoughts and emotions align with your intentions, you create a resonance that amplifies your energy and draws opportunities into your life.

One real-world example is the global meditation experiments conducted by organizations like the HeartMath Institute. In these studies, large groups of people meditated on feelings of love and peace, measuring the effects on global coherence. Remarkably, during these synchronized efforts, researchers observed reductions in local violence and increases in social harmony. This is resonance at work— individual frequencies combining to create a wave of positive change.

## Tuning to Your Intentions

Think of your intentions as musical notes. When they are clear and focused, they resonate deeply, creating harmonics that extend into the quantum field. But when they are scattered or conflicted, their power diminishes. Aligning your thoughts, emotions, and actions with a singular intention allows you to create a resonance that magnifies your efforts.

Consider the story of an entrepreneur who visualizes their dream business daily. Each morning, they aligned their thoughts by imagining the details of their success—the people they would serve and the impact they would create. This clarity of intention resonated with their actions, guiding them to opportunities and collaborators who shared their vision. Over time, their focused resonance transformed a dream into reality.

Then there is **Saanvi Dogra**. Deeply passionate about science education, she envisioned creating opportunities for underserved children worldwide. She dedicated herself to this mission, focusing her energy and intentions on making a tangible impact. Through her commitment, Saanvi founded Science Nexus, a nonprofit organization aimed at furthering inclusive science education for underserved children globally. By mobilizing a network of over 70 volunteers and fostering collaborations with various organizations and under-resourced schools,

Science Nexus has successfully provided hands-on science projects to students who previously lacked such opportunities.

---

## Reflective Exercise: Aligning with Your Frequency

Close your eyes and take a deep breath. Imagine your intention as a single note resonating in your heart. As you exhale, visualize this note extending outward, harmonizing with the vibrations of the universe. Feel its energy growing stronger, drawing opportunities, people, and circumstances that align with your vision. Breathe deeply and carry this resonance into your day, knowing that your aligned frequency amplifies your ability to create.

---

## Resonance and Relationships

Resonance also plays a profound role in our connections with others. Have you ever met someone whose energy seemed to align perfectly with yours? This feeling of connection often stems from shared frequencies—similar values, intentions, or emotional states. When two people resonate, their energies amplify each other, creating a bond that feels effortless and powerful.

Conversely, relationships marked by discord often reflect mismatched frequencies. By aligning our energy with love, compassion, and understanding, we can create resonance even in challenging interactions, transforming dissonance into harmony.

## Resonance as a Spiritual Practice

In spiritual traditions, resonance is often described as aligning with the divine. Prayer, meditation, and acts of kindness are ways to tune our frequencies to higher vibrations, creating resonance with the universe. This alignment not only amplifies our intentions but also deepens our connection to the sacred, reminding us of our role in the greater symphony of existence.

---

## Reflective Exercise: Creating Resonance in Your Life

As you move through your day, pause to notice the frequencies you are projecting. Are your thoughts and emotions aligned with your intentions? Are your actions resonating with the life you wish to create? Take a moment to adjust your frequency, tuning into gratitude, love, or purpose. As you do, feel the resonance building within you, amplifying your energy and drawing the symphony of the universe closer to your heart.

---

Through resonance, we discover the power of alignment. It is the force that amplifies our intentions, connects us to others, and harmonizes us with the quantum field. When we tune ourselves to higher frequencies, we become instruments of creation, playing our part in the universal melody.

## Solfeggio Frequencies: Sound as a Tool for Alignment

Close your eyes for a moment and imagine a deep, resonant tone washing over you. Its vibration feels ancient, almost otherworldly as if it carries the secrets of creation within its sound. This is the essence of Solfeggio frequencies, a set of tones believed to hold profound healing and harmonizing properties. These frequencies, rooted in sacred traditions, offer a powerful way to align with the universe's natural rhythms and elevate our connection to the quantum field.

Solfeggio frequencies are specific sound frequencies believed to have healing properties and spiritual significance. These frequencies are said to align with ancient musical scales and resonate with the natural vibration of the universe, promoting harmony, balance, and well-being in those who listen.

### The Ancient Origins of Solfeggio Frequencies

The Solfeggio frequencies trace their origins to Gregorian chants sung by monks during meditation and prayer. These chants were composed using specific tones, each associated with a particular frequency. Unlike modern musical scales, these frequencies were said to have unique vibrational qualities, capable of promoting spiritual awakening, emotional healing, and physical well-being.

One of the most well-known frequencies is 528 Hz, often referred to as the "Love Frequency." It is believed to resonate with the vibration of love, DNA repair, and transformation. Whether myth or measurable science, the power of these tones lies in their ability to create resonance within the listener, aligning their energy with higher states of consciousness.

> **Rediscovery:** Dr. Joseph Puleo, in the 1970s, identified six core Solfeggio frequencies within biblical texts and ancient numerology, linking them to specific healing and transformative properties.

## The Science of Sound and Vibration

Sound is not just a sensory experience; it is a form of energy that interacts with matter and consciousness. Modern research shows that specific frequencies can influence brainwaves, promoting states of relaxation, focus, and even healing. Binaural beats, for example, use two slightly different frequencies in each ear to create a third tone in the brain, aligning brainwaves to specific states.

On a physical level, sound waves can influence water molecules, a phenomenon demonstrated by **Masaru Emoto's** experiments on the impact of music and intention on water crystals. Given that our bodies are mostly water, it's no surprise that sound has profound effects on our energy and well-being.

## Using Solfeggio Frequencies for Alignment

Incorporating Solfeggio frequencies into daily practice can help align your energy with the quantum field. You can find recordings of these tones online, often paired with meditative music or nature sounds. To experience their effects, find a quiet space, close your eyes, and focus on the tone as it fills your awareness. Allow its vibration to resonate through your body, harmonizing your energy with its frequency.

---

### Reflective Exercise: Tuning Into Solfeggio Frequencies

Choose a frequency that resonates with your current intention. For example, 396 Hz is associated with liberating guilt and fear, while 741 Hz promotes intuition and clarity. As you listen, visualize the frequency as a wave of light moving through you, clearing away blockages and aligning your energy with your desired state. Feel its vibration merging with your own, creating harmony within and around you.

---

### | *Stories of Transformation Through Sound* |

The healing power of sound is not confined to ancient traditions; it continues to touch lives today. Consider the story of Martha, a 53-year-old stage 3 breast cancer survivor who used sound therapy as part of her healing journey. She shared that attending gong sound healing meditations made her feel *"completely relaxed,"* as if she were *"being transported to another dimension for an hour."* This alignment was a key part of her recovery.

Another example comes from schools using Solfeggio tones in classrooms to help students focus and reduce stress. Teachers have reported calmer, more engaged students, reflecting the harmonizing effects of these frequencies on group dynamics.

## Sound as a Bridge to the Divine

Solfeggio frequencies remind us that sound is more than vibration; it is a bridge between the physical and the spiritual. Whether through chanting, music, or silent prayer, sound connects us to the divine symphony of the universe, tuning our energy to the higher frequencies of love, healing, and creation.

As we continue this journey, consider how the power of sound can deepen your connection to the quantum field. The symphony is already playing; all you need to do is tune in.

# Cosmic Harmony: The Interconnected Balance of Existence

Close your eyes for a moment and imagine the night sky. Stars twinkle in the vast expanse, seemingly scattered in randomness, yet each one holds its place within a larger design. These celestial bodies orbit, align, and interact with precision, guided by invisible forces of gravity and motion. This cosmic dance is not chaos; it is harmony—a delicate interplay of energies that reflects the interconnected balance of existence.

## The Cosmic Web

At the largest scales, the universe resembles a vast web, where galaxies are the nodes and invisible strands of energy connect everything. This structure, often called the "cosmic web," is a testament to the interdependence of all things. Each galaxy's movement is influenced by countless others, creating a symphony of gravitational interplay. Just as a single note in a melody can elevate the whole piece, each component of the universe contributes to its overarching harmony.

On Earth, this principle is mirrored in ecosystems, where the balance of life depends on the interconnectedness of species. The extinction of a single organism can disrupt an entire ecosystem, just as a discordant note can jar the beauty of a symphony. In both cases, harmony emerges from connection—a delicate alignment of energies working together for the greater whole.

## Harmony in Human Experience

This interconnected balance extends beyond the physical and into the realm of human experience. Consider the ways in which our actions, thoughts, and emotions ripple outward, affecting not only ourselves but also those around us. A kind word, like a single star in the night sky, can light up the lives of others, creating a chain reaction of positivity and connection.

### | *A Story of Harmony in Action* |

One powerful example comes from the story of **Desmond Tutu** and **Nelson Mandela**, whose shared vision of reconciliation and peace transformed the social fabric of South Africa. Their belief in unity, even in the face of division, resonated with millions, creating a wave of change that echoed far beyond their lifetimes. Their actions remind us that when individuals align their energies with love and compassion, they contribute to a greater harmony that uplifts the collective.

---

## Reflective Exercise: Feeling the Cosmic Connection

Take a moment to sit quietly. Imagine yourself as a single star in the vast expanse of the universe. Feel the energy flowing through you, connecting you to every other star, every planet, every being. With each breath, picture the invisible threads of connection growing stronger, weaving you into the fabric of existence. As you exhale, send out a vibration of gratitude, knowing that your energy contributes to the harmony of the whole.

---

## Resonance Across Dimensions

The idea of cosmic harmony extends to the quantum level, where particles exist not as isolated entities but as part of a unified field. Quantum entanglement demonstrates this beautifully: when two particles become entangled, their states remain linked, no matter how far apart they are. Change one, and the other responds instantaneously. This phenomenon hints at a deeper truth—the universe is not a collection of separate parts but an interconnected whole, where every action reverberates through the field.

In our daily lives, we experience this interconnectedness in subtle ways. Have you ever thought about a friend, only for them to call moments later? Or felt a wave of calm when someone silently prayed for you? These moments remind us that the energy we put into the world has the power to resonate across space and time, connecting us to others in ways we cannot always see.

## The Symphony of Creation

The universe itself is a symphony composed of countless instruments playing in perfect balance. From the vibrations of atoms to the gravitational waves rippling through space, every element of existence contributes to this grand melody. As co-creators within this symphony, our role is not passive; it is participatory. By aligning our thoughts, emotions, and actions with the higher frequencies of love, gratitude, and compassion, we join the chorus, adding our unique voice to the cosmic song.

---

## Reflective Exercise: Adding Your Voice to the Symphony

Close your eyes and imagine the universe as a great orchestra, each star and planet playing its part. Picture yourself as an instrument within this ensemble. What note are you playing? Is it one of joy, fear, or love? Take a deep breath, and as you exhale, tune your energy to a frequency of harmony and gratitude. Feel your note blending with the others, creating a melody that echoes across time and space.

---

Cosmic harmony teaches us that life is not a solitary journey but a shared experience, where each action and intention contributes to the balance of the whole. Whether through the stars above, the ecosystems around us, or the quantum field within, the universe reminds us of our profound connection to all that is.

And as we embrace this interconnectedness, we discover that we are not just observers of the symphony—we are its co-creators.

# Revisiting the Core Concepts and Insights

**Harmony**, as it turns out, is not just a pleasing concept—it is the fundamental order of existence. In the quantum field, particles moving in perfect coherence reveal a truth that resonates far beyond the subatomic. When states align, potential amplifies, and what seemed fragmented becomes whole. This coherence is not limited to physics; it speaks to the way our thoughts, emotions, and actions can unify into a focused energy that transforms chaos into clarity.

**Resonance** carries this energy further, like a tuning fork setting another into motion without touch. It is the unseen force that amplifies our intentions, connecting them to opportunities and outcomes in ways that feel almost magical. But resonance is not magic—it is alignment. When a thought is pure, when an emotion is steady, when an action follows with purpose, the vibration spreads outward, rippling through the field. It is the reason a kind word can change a day, a shared vision can change a life, and a collective intention can ripple through the world.

Sound, too, reminds us of this invisible order. **Solfeggio frequencies**, ancient and deeply resonant, demonstrate how vibration shapes energy. A single tone can calm a restless mind or ignite a deep sense of purpose. These frequencies are not simply heard—they are felt, aligning the listener with higher vibrations of healing and creation. When sound interacts with water, as seen in experiments shaping intricate crystalline patterns, it reflects the deeper truth of how vibration organizes life itself. And we, being composed of so much water, resonate with these tones, finding harmony within and without.

The vastness of **cosmic harmony** brings it all together. The universe, from its stars to its smallest particles, dances in synchrony. Galaxies spiral in perfect rhythm, ecosystems thrive in delicate balance, and even our relationships reflect this interconnected song. Harmony is not something the universe strives for—it is what the universe is. And in this grand melody, our own contributions matter. A single thought, a single act of love, a single moment of alignment adds to the symphony. It reminds us that existence is not isolated chaos but an intricate, interwoven masterpiece.

Every step in this journey points to the same truth: alignment is power. Whether through coherence, resonance, sound, or cosmic balance, the universe reflects what we offer. When we align ourselves with its frequencies of love, gratitude, and purpose, we amplify our ability to create, connect, and thrive. The symphony plays on, and each of us holds an instrument, waiting to join the song.

...

The interconnected harmony of the universe feels deeply familiar, as though whispered through the ages by ancient sages and mystics. Sacred traditions have long hinted at this universal balance, embedding their wisdom in symbols, stories, and teachings. What happens when we view these timeless truths through the lens of modern quantum discoveries?

The path ahead leads to a fascinating convergence of the sacred and the scientific, revealing how ancient wisdom and modern understanding are part of the same eternal melody.

# Chapter Four

# Bridging Ancient Wisdom and Modern Science

*"Faith is to believe what you do not see; the reward of this faith is to see what you believe."*

— Saint Augustine

Imagine standing before a temple carved into the side of a mountain, its intricate patterns telling stories of creation, harmony, and balance. These geometric designs, precise yet timeless, are not merely decorations—they are reflections of universal truths. Now, step into a modern laboratory where cutting-edge quantum experiments reveal patterns of symmetry, order, and interconnectedness. At first glance, these two worlds might seem far apart, but look closely, and you'll find that their stories echo the same profound message: the universe is a masterpiece of design, and we are part of its intricate fabric.

From the sacred geometry etched into temples to the equations of quantum mechanics, humanity has long sought to understand the order behind existence. The timeless truths of spiritual traditions and the groundbreaking discoveries of quantum physics often mirror one another, revealing a shared narrative about the interconnected nature of reality. By delving into these parallels, we uncover a holistic view that unites the spiritual and the scientific.

## Sacred Geometry: Universal Patterns of Order

Picture a snowflake, its crystalline structure branching outward in perfect symmetry, or the spiral of a seashell that mirrors the curvature of galaxies. These patterns are not coincidences; they are expressions of a deeper order, one that has fascinated humans for millennia. *Sacred geometry,* as it has come to be known, is the study of these universal patterns, believed to be the blueprint of creation itself.

This concept is not limited to temples and mandalas; it resonates across cultures. Consider the dot paintings of Indigenous Australian art, which depict the interconnected web of the Dreamtime. Each dot and line signifies a connection, echoing the patterns seen in sacred geometry and the quantum field, where particles remain linked across vast distances.

> **Sacred Geometry** is the study of special shapes, patterns, and designs that appear in nature and ancient art, which people believe hold spiritual meaning and energy. These patterns, like circles, spirals, and the Flower of Life, are thought to represent the building blocks of the universe and connect all of creation.

## The Language of the Universe

Ancient cultures revered these patterns, embedding them in their art, architecture, and spiritual practices. The Pyramids of Egypt, Stonehenge, and the mandalas of Eastern traditions all reflect an understanding of geometric harmony. The circle, square, and triangle—simple shapes—were seen as symbols of wholeness, balance, and the divine. These forms were not just artistic choices; they were believed to carry the essence of universal truths.

Modern science, in its quest to decode the fabric of reality, has uncovered striking parallels. The *Fibonacci sequence,* for example, appears in everything from the arrangement of leaves on a stem to the proportions of the human body. At the quantum level, particles exhibit symmetrical behaviors, adhering to mathematical principles that mirror the harmony seen in sacred geometry. It is as though the same hand that shaped the cosmos also inscribed its patterns into the smallest details of life.

## The Flower of Life

One of the most recognized symbols in sacred geometry is the *Flower of Life,* a pattern of overlapping circles that forms a complex, interconnected design. Similarly, the Sri Yantra in Hindu tradition represents the intricate balance between opposing forces, such as the masculine and feminine. Its geometry mirrors the patterns found in the quantum field, where symmetry and balance guide the behavior of particles and energy.. Found in

*The Flower of Life*

ancient temples across the world, this symbol is said to represent the interconnectedness of all life. Its geometry is not just aesthetically pleasing—it encodes mathematical relationships that underpin the physical universe.

***Imagine this:*** the atoms in your body, the structure of a galaxy, and the notes in a symphony all follow patterns that can be traced back to the principles found in the Flower of Life. It is a reminder that existence is not random but intricately woven together, a masterpiece of design.

## Reflections in Nature

Nature itself is a testament to sacred geometry. Look closely at the veins of a leaf, the spiral of a hurricane, or the branching of a tree, and you'll see these patterns repeated over and over. Fractals, such as those found in river systems or the structure of broccoli, embody this repeating complexity within simplicity. These self-similar patterns reflect the ability of the universe to scale infinite detail from basic principles—a reminder that sacred geometry is written into the fabric of existence.

Even water, when frozen, reveals hexagonal crystals—a phenomenon so delicate that even slight disruptions in energy can alter their structure. This sensitivity to vibration is a clue to the deeper connections between geometry, energy, and intention, as explored by researchers like Masaru Emoto, who demonstrated how positive words and emotions influenced the crystalline patterns of water.

## Sacred Geometry and the Quantum Field

In the quantum field, patterns of symmetry and balance govern the behavior of particles. These principles echo the ancient understanding of sacred geometry as a reflection of divine order. Just as a mandala invites meditation and alignment, the symmetries of the quantum world invite awe and reflection on the interconnected nature of existence.

Consider how particles follow pathways that create symmetrical interference patterns in double-slit experiments. These patterns are not random; they are evidence of an underlying order, one that suggests the presence of a universal design. Sacred geometry bridges the ancient understanding of divine harmony with modern discoveries in quantum mechanics, where patterns of symmetry govern the building blocks of reality.

---

## Reflective Exercise: Recognizing Patterns in Your Life

Take a moment to think about the patterns in your own life. Are there recurring themes, shapes, or relationships that seem to guide your path? Close your eyes and visualize a mandala, its intricate design unfolding like the petals of a flower. With each breath, imagine yourself aligning with the order and balance it represents. As you open your eyes, consider how you can bring greater harmony into your thoughts, actions, and relationships.

---

Sacred geometry reminds us that the universe is not chaotic but beautifully ordered, with patterns that guide everything from the motion of galaxies to the flow of our daily lives. It invites us to see ourselves not as isolated fragments but as integral parts of a grand design woven into the fabric of existence. And as we explore this design further, we uncover the timeless truths that connect ancient wisdom to modern science.

# Universal Truths: Foundational Spiritual Principles Mirrored in Quantum Mechanics

In the quiet halls of ancient temples and the meticulous equations of modern laboratories lies a shared pursuit: uncovering the truths that govern existence. While one path seeks enlightenment through spiritual reflection and the other through empirical discovery, they often converge, pointing to the same foundational principles. These universal truths—*interconnection, intention,* and *transformation* — are as much the domain of mystics as they are of quantum physicists.

> **Quantum Mechanics** is a fundamental theory used to describe the behavior of nature at and below atomic scale. It is the foundation of all quantum physics: quantum chemistry, quantum field theory, quantum technology, and quantum information science.

### Interconnection: The Thread That Binds

Quantum entanglement provides a scientific parallel to spiritual teachings of interconnectedness. Particles separated by vast distances respond to one another instantaneously, mirroring the spiritual understanding that all life is bound by an invisible web of energy.

Indigenous wisdom speaks of the Earth as a living being, where every action ripples through the whole. Buddhism describes the "interdependent origination," where nothing exists independently but arises through relationships. This idea is also reflected in the Adinkra symbols of Ghana, which embody profound philosophical concepts of unity and connection. For example, the symbol 'Eban' signifies safety and protection, emphasizing the sheltering relationships between individuals and their communities. Adinkra patterns are not only cultural artifacts but carry layers of meaning that resonate with the principles of harmony and unity across existence. Modern physicists have even identified parallels between these symbols and the mathematical frameworks of supersymmetry, suggesting that such ancient wisdom encapsulates universal truths about interconnectedness.

These cultural and spiritual insights echo the discoveries of quantum entanglement, where particles, once connected, remain linked across vast distances. Change one, and the other responds instantly, as though the fabric of reality itself refuses separation. Like the Adinkra symbols etched into fabric and walls, the universe itself seems to weave an intricate, interconnected design where every part influences the whole.

Imagine two people separated by thousands of miles yet feeling an inexplicable synchronicity—calling each other at the same moment or sharing the same thought. Quantum physics offers a framework for this mystery: the connections in the quantum field do not recognize space as a boundary. In the same way, spiritual truths remind us that we are not isolated islands but threads in an infinite tapestry.

## Intention: The Creative Force

In the scriptures of nearly every tradition lies the belief that thought and intention shape reality. *"As a man thinketh in his heart, so is he,"* declares Proverbs 23:7 Prayer, meditation, and rituals are practices of focused intention, directing the mind's energy toward a desired outcome. Quantum mechanics, through the observer effect, shows us that observation itself influences the behavior of particles, collapsing waves of potential into reality. It is as if the universe waits for direction, responding to the intention of its participants.

This interplay between thought and reality is not abstract; it is deeply personal. Consider a farmer who plants a seed with hope, envisioning the harvest before the first sprout appears. The farmer's care, belief, and effort are forms of intention, shaping the growth of the seed into sustenance. In quantum terms, the seed represents a field of potential, while the farmer's intention collapses that potential into form.

## Transformation: The Eternal Cycle

From ancient alchemy to modern particle physics, the principle of transformation lies at the heart of existence. Spiritual traditions teach that change is not destruction but renewal. The phoenix rising from its ashes, the soul's journey through reincarnation, and the transformation of suffering into wisdom all reflect this truth. Quantum mechanics, too, reveals a universe in constant flux. Particles transform into waves and back again, energy becomes matter, and chaos gives birth to order.

Imagine a caterpillar spinning its cocoon, surrendering itself to a process of dissolution before emerging as a butterfly. This cycle of transformation mirrors the quantum dance of energy and matter, where change is not an end but a beginning. The same principle applies to our lives, where moments of struggle often precede profound growth.

Transformation is not a failure of stability—it is the engine of creation.

## Bridging Ancient Wisdom and Modern Discovery

What makes these truths so remarkable is their consistency across time and disciplines. Whether through sacred texts or scientific studies, they reveal a universe governed by harmony and purpose. The interconnectedness of quantum particles mirrors the spiritual web of life. The creative power of intention aligns with the observer effect. The transformative nature of energy and matter echoes the cycles of spiritual growth.

Each truth invites us to participate consciously in the unfolding of reality. When we recognize our interconnection, we act with greater compassion. When we direct our intentions, we shape the potential of the quantum field. When we embrace transformation, we align with the creative flow of the universe. These principles are not abstract—they are practical, guiding us to live with awareness, purpose, and harmony.

---

### Reflective Exercise: Aligning with Universal Truths

Find a quiet space and close your eyes. Reflect on the connections in your life—relationships, experiences, and even challenges that have shaped who you are. Imagine these connections as threads of light forming a vast web around you. Now, focus on a single intention, something you wish to create or transform.

Visualize it clearly, feeling the energy of your intention rippling through the web. With each breath, embrace the changes required to bring this intention to life, knowing that transformation is a natural part of the process.

---

The universal truths revealed by ancient wisdom and quantum mechanics remind us that we are both participants in and co-creators of reality. They are the bridge between the spiritual and the scientific, guiding us to a deeper understanding of our place in the cosmos. As we continue this journey, we turn to the symbols and metaphors of scripture, finding reflections of these truths in the stories that have shaped human thought for millennia.

## Symbolism in Scripture: Metaphors for Quantum Ideas

Throughout history, sacred texts have used vivid metaphors to illuminate the mysteries of existence. These stories, poems, and parables are more than ancient teachings—they are keys encoded with wisdom about the nature of reality. What's striking is how many of these symbols align with discoveries in quantum physics. It's as if the authors of scripture glimpsed truths that science is only now beginning to understand, their metaphors pointing us to the interplay between the spiritual and the quantum.

### The Light That Connects All Things

*"In the beginning was the Word, and the Word was with God, and the Word was God."* This opening passage from the Gospel of John speaks of Logos, the divine principle of order and reason. Yet, as the story unfolds, the Word becomes Light, a force that shines in the darkness. In spiritual terms, Light symbolizes divine connection and truth. In quantum terms, light is something even more extraordinary—both a particle and a wave, a form of energy that defies easy categorization. It is the carrier of information, the means by which the universe communicates across time and space.

Think of the double-slit experiment, where photons of light behave as particles when observed and as waves when left undisturbed. The experiment reveals not only the dual nature of light but also the role of the observer in shaping its behavior. The metaphor of divine Light in scripture parallels this idea, suggesting that creation responds to awareness and that the act of seeing itself shapes what is seen.

> **Double-slit Experiment:** Light or particles (such as electrons) are sent through two slits onto a screen. When unobserved, they create an interference pattern on the screen, behaving like waves that overlap. When scientists place a measuring device to observe which slit the particle passes through, the interference pattern disappears, and the particles behave as if they are solid objects (particles) traveling through one slit or the other.

## The Seed and the Field

Many spiritual traditions speak of seeds, small and unassuming, that hold the potential for life. *"The kingdom of heaven is like a mustard seed,"* Jesus tells his followers, *"which is the smallest of all seeds but grows into the largest of garden plants."* The seed is a metaphor for potential, a microcosm containing everything needed to become something far greater. Similarly, the quantum field is often described as a sea of potential—a space where particles, like seeds, exist in countless possible states until observed.

Picture a farmer scattering seeds into fertile soil, each one a tiny universe of possibility. The farmer's care, intention, and faith in the unseen process reflect the quantum principle of collapsing potential into reality. The seed's transformation into a plant mirrors the way particles emerge from the quantum field, brought into being through alignment and attention.

## The Ladder to Higher Realities

In the Book of Genesis, Jacob dreams of a ladder reaching from Earth to Heaven, with angels ascending and descending its rungs. The ladder symbolizes a connection between realms—a path linking the physical and the divine. In quantum physics, there is a similar concept: the idea that energy levels exist as discrete steps. Electrons don't slide smoothly from one state to another; they "jump" between levels, existing briefly in a superposition of states before resolving into one.

The metaphor of Jacob's ladder reminds us that spiritual growth, like quantum change, happens in leaps. Moments of transformation are not gradual but sudden, as if we are lifted to a higher vibration. The story invites reflection: What steps are you climbing in your own journey? And how do those steps align with the quantum leaps of your inner potential?

## The Web of Life

Eastern traditions often describe the universe as a great web, where each thread connects to every other. The Vedas of India speak of Indra's net, a vast lattice adorned with jewels, each reflecting the light of all others. This vision of interconnectedness mirrors the quantum phenomenon of entanglement, where particles remain linked regardless of distance. Change one, and the other responds instantaneously, as though the separation between them is an illusion.

In our lives, the metaphor of the web invites us to consider how our actions, thoughts, and intentions ripple outward. A kind gesture, like a single vibration on a thread, travels far beyond its origin, touching lives we may never meet. The quantum entanglement described by physics reveals a similar truth: the boundaries we perceive are not as solid as they seem.

## Reflective Exercise: Finding Your Place in the Story

Close your eyes and imagine yourself within a great story. You are the seed, holding infinite potential. You are the light shining into the darkness. You are the traveler on the ladder, reaching higher with each step. And you are the jewel in the web, reflecting and amplifying the beauty of others. As you breathe deeply, consider how these metaphors resonate in your own life. What potential are you nurturing? What connections are you strengthening? And how can you align your story with the greater symphony of the universe?

## Scripture as a Bridge

These ancient symbols and stories, born from a time before quantum mechanics, carry an uncanny resonance with modern science. They remind us that the quest to understand the universe is not new—it is a timeless journey, one that blends observation with imagination and analysis with faith. Sacred texts, whether describing the Tao's infinite source or Indra's net of interconnected jewels, resonate with the discoveries of quantum physics, where every particle reflects the whole and every connection contributes to the greater unity. And as we contemplate these metaphors, we find ourselves standing at the threshold of something even more profound—the Logos, the principle that weaves it all together.

## Logos: The Divine Principle of Reason and Order

There is a word—ancient, profound, and timeless—that echoes through scripture, philosophy, and even the discoveries of modern science: Logos. To the Greeks, Logos was reason, the underlying logic that governed the cosmos. To the early Christians, it was the divine Word through which all creation was made. Across cultures, Logos represents the principle of order in a seemingly chaotic universe. It is the thread that ties the infinite to the finite, the Creator to creation, and the spiritual to the scientific.

## The Logos and the Fabric of Creation

*"In the beginning was the Word, and the Word was with God, and the Word was God."* This passage from the Gospel of John reverberates with significance. It declares that creation itself is not random but born of intention and reason. Logos, the divine Word, is described as the blueprint of all existence, the ordering force that brings chaos into harmony. Modern science offers a fascinating parallel in the holographic universe hypothesis, which suggests that the three-dimensional reality we perceive is a projection from a two-dimensional surface. Much like the ancient idea of Logos, this theory points to an underlying structure that organizes creation.

In modern terms, the quantum field can be seen as an echo of this principle. The field is a sea of endless potential, yet within it lies an implicit order. Particles move in patterns of symmetry, energy transforms with precision, and even the seemingly random follows the laws of probability. Logos is not only the spark of creation—it is the order that sustains it, ensuring the universe remains coherent, purposeful, and alive.

## The Cosmic Dance of Order and Chaos

Imagine an artist standing before a blank canvas. To the untrained eye, the canvas is chaos—an undefined void waiting for meaning. But to the artist, it is filled with potential, each brushstroke guided by an unseen vision. Logos is the artist's hand, turning possibility into reality, shaping the canvas of the universe into something beautiful and meaningful.

In quantum mechanics, this interplay between chaos and order is evident. Particles exist in superpositions, their states undefined until observed. Yet, when measured, they resolve into precise forms as if following an unseen script. This phenomenon mirrors the ancient understanding of Logos: the universe is both infinite potential and meticulous order, a dance between the unknowable and the known.

## Logos in the Natural World

The natural world is a testament to the presence of Logos. From the spirals of a nautilus shell to the orbits of planets, patterns emerge that reflect harmony and reason. Consider the golden ratio, a mathematical proportion found in everything from sunflowers to galaxies. This ratio is not arbitrary; it is the fingerprint of Logos, a reminder that creation follows divine logic.

Even the cycles of life—birth, growth, decay, and renewal—are guided by this principle. Recent discoveries in quantum computing suggest that error correction codes are woven into spacetime itself, ensuring the universe's stability and coherence. These findings echo the idea of Logos as the sustaining force of balance and harmony, showing how order emerges from chaos on the most fundamental levels. Trees shed their leaves, rivers carve paths through stone, and seasons shift with precision. Logos weaves these cycles together, ensuring that life continues in balance and harmony. The laws of nature, whether described by spiritual traditions or scientific formulas, are expressions of the same divine order.

## Human Consciousness and the Logos

As beings of consciousness, we are uniquely attuned to Logos. Our capacity for reason, creativity, and reflection allows us to recognize the patterns and principles that govern existence. When we align with Logos, we participate in the act of creation, bringing harmony to our lives and the world around us.

Consider the moments when everything seems to "click," when your thoughts, emotions, and actions align seamlessly. These moments are not accidents—they are instances of resonance with the divine order. By living with intention, we align ourselves with Logos, becoming co-creators in the unfolding of the universe.

---

## Reflective Exercise: Aligning with Logos

Close your eyes and take a deep breath. Imagine the universe as a great symphony, each note perfectly placed, each instrument playing its part. Now, picture yourself as a note within this symphony. Ask yourself: What is my purpose? What harmony can I contribute? As you breathe, feel the rhythm of your life aligning with the greater order, your actions guided by the wisdom of Logos.

---

## The Logos as the Bridge

Logos bridges the spiritual and the scientific, manifesting in the design of cathedrals that reflect celestial harmony or in the equations of modern physics that reveal order in chaos. By aligning our lives with this divine principle, we contribute to the coherence of creation. It reminds us that the universe is not a collection of random events but a masterpiece of design. Whether we encounter this principle through scripture, nature, or the quantum field, it invites us to marvel at the coherence of existence. As we align with Logos, we discover our role in the divine story—a story that continues to unfold with every breath, every thought, and every act of creation.

## Reflective Exercise: Aligning Logos with Daily Life

Close your eyes and visualize a fractal pattern emerging within your mind—a single, self-repeating design that grows infinitely. As you reflect on this pattern, consider how your thoughts and actions align with the order it represents. What choices can you make today to reflect this balance in your relationships, work, and inner world?

## Revisiting the Core Concepts and Insights

Order, harmony, and connection lie at the heart of both ancient wisdom and modern science. They speak through patterns etched in sacred geometry, truths whispered in scripture, and principles illuminated by quantum discoveries. They tell a story of a universe that is not chaotic but purposeful—a masterpiece woven from the threads of reason and intention.

**Sacred geometry** reminds us that the universe is built on a foundation of design. The shapes and patterns found in the natural world echo through ancient temples and modern equations, revealing the language of creation. Whether in the symmetry of a honeycomb, the spiral of a galaxy, or the Flower of Life, these patterns reflect a divine order that connects all things.

**Universal truths**, shared across spiritual traditions and quantum mechanics, highlight the interconnected nature of existence. Particles entangled across vast distances behave as though they are one. Similarly, spiritual teachings remind us that we are never separate but part of an intricate web of relationships. Intention—the creative force of thought—shapes reality, whether through the prayers of the faithful or the observer effect of quantum experiments. Transformation, too, bridges these worlds, showing us that change is not destruction but the pathway to renewal.

**Scriptural metaphors** illuminate these truths with profound simplicity. A seed contains the infinite potential of a tree, much like particles in the quantum field hold countless possibilities. Light, both a wave and a particle, reflects divine truth and creation. The ladder of Jacob, the net of Indra, and countless other symbols offer timeless insights that mirror the quantum understanding of leaps, connection, and harmony.

Finally, the concept of **Logos** ties everything together, offering a principle that unites the spiritual and the scientific. It is the divine Word, the reasoning behind existence, and the order that sustains creation. Logos reminds us that the universe is not random but guided by an unseen intelligence, one that we are invited to align with. When we live in harmony with this principle, our lives reflect the same balance and coherence that governs the stars.

These insights are not distant ideas but invitations. They call us to see the sacred in the patterns of a leaf, to recognize our power to shape reality through intention, and to marvel at the interconnected web that binds us to everything else. They remind us that we are part of something vast and beautiful, a symphony of creation that sings with the voice of Logos.

...

The principles of sacred geometry, universal truths, and Logos all point to one profound realization: the universe responds to intention. But how do we practically engage with this knowledge? How can we use the tools of thought, prayer, and trust to shape the quantum field and bring our visions into reality?

The next step in this journey moves from understanding to action, exploring how to turn potential into manifestation and align ourselves with the creative forces of the universe.

# Chapter Five

# The Mechanics of Manifestation

*"When you want something, all the universe conspires in helping you to achieve it."*

– Paulo Coelho

Imagine holding a painter's brush, poised over a blank canvas. The colors are endless, and the possibilities stretch as far as your imagination. Now, picture the canvas as your life, the brush as your mind, and the quantum field as the palette from which you draw. Every thought, every intention, every focused moment becomes a stroke in the masterpiece of your reality. This is not just a metaphor—it is the profound interplay of mind and matter in action.

In this chapter, we step into the practical world of manifestation, where thought shapes reality and intention aligns with the quantum field. Just as a sculptor carves stone to reveal form, you can use specific tools and principles to shape the potential of your life into something tangible. We'll explore how focusing your thoughts, embracing practices like prayer and meditation, and trusting in unseen mechanisms allow you to influence the world around you.

## Intentionality – Focusing Thought to Shape Reality

### The Power of a Single Thought

Pause for a moment and think of a pebble dropped into a still pond. The ripple spreads outward, touching every inch of the water's surface, even long after the pebble sinks. Intentionality works the same way. A single focused thought, infused with clarity and purpose, can ripple out into the quantum field, influencing outcomes far beyond what you might imagine.

But what makes intention so powerful? The answer lies in its ability to align your energy with your desires. Just as a laser focuses light to create precision and power, your mind focuses thought to create resonance in the quantum field. Intentionality is not merely wishing or hoping—it is the deliberate act of choosing a thought, directing your energy, and believing in its impact.

## Clarity: The Foundation of Intention

Imagine entering a pitch-black room and fumbling for the light switch. Without clarity, your actions are scattered, and progress is slow. The same is true for your intentions.

Consider the sand paintings of the Navajo people, created in sacred ceremonies to bring healing and balance. Each line, color, and symbol is chosen with deliberate intention, representing harmony between the physical and spiritual realms. Much like these intricate designs, your intentions are most powerful when focused and deliberate, aligning with the universal energy that surrounds you.

To shape reality, your thoughts must be clear, specific, and focused. Instead of saying, "I want to be successful," define what success looks like—perhaps it's starting your own business, writing a book, or improving your relationships. Clarity gives your intention direction, much like a GPS guides a traveler to their destination.

## Energy Follows Thought

In both spirituality and quantum physics, there is a profound principle: energy flows where attention goes. When you focus on a goal or desire, you direct your mental and emotional energy toward it, creating resonance in the field. This alignment sets off a chain reaction, attracting opportunities, people, and circumstances that match your vibration.

Consider the story of an Olympic athlete who trains for years, visualizing every movement, every finish line. Their focused intention not only guides their physical training but also aligns their mental state with the outcome they seek. When they achieve victory, it feels almost inevitable—a natural result of years of focused thought and action working in harmony.

---

## Reflection Exercise: Defining Your Intentions

Take a moment to sit quietly and think about an area of your life you want to improve. Close your eyes and ask yourself: What does success look like here? Be specific. If it's financial abundance, imagine the exact amount you want to earn. If it's health, visualize yourself vibrant and energetic. Write down your intention as a clear, concise statement. By giving your intention form, you take the first step toward manifesting it in reality.

---

## Overcoming Mental Noise

A clear intention can be disrupted by doubt, fear, or conflicting thoughts. These mental "noises" act like static on a radio signal, distorting your connection with the quantum field. Learning to quiet these doubts is essential for maintaining the integrity of your intention. This is where practices like meditation and mindfulness come into play, helping you cultivate a state of focused calm where your thoughts can resonate clearly.

## Living with Purpose

Intentionality goes beyond manifesting specific goals—it is a way of living. When you approach each day with purpose, aligning your actions with your values and desires, you create a life that reflects your true self. This is where the quantum field responds most powerfully, not to fleeting whims but to sustained, authentic energy.

Intentionality is the foundation of manifestation. It is the first step in a process that transforms thought into reality, setting the stage for deeper practices like prayer, meditation, and visualization. As you master this art, you'll find that the quantum field responds in ways that feel almost miraculous, aligning your inner world with the outer reality you wish to create. And as we move forward, we'll explore how timeless practices like prayer and meditation serve as bridges to the field, amplifying the power of your intentions.

## Prayer and Meditation — Tools for Aligning with the Quantum Field

Picture this: you're sitting quietly in the stillness of a morning. The world hasn't fully woken up yet, and the air feels charged with possibility. You close your eyes and take a deep breath, exhaling the weight of yesterday. In that moment, your thoughts begin to settle, and a feeling of connection washes over you. This isn't just relaxation; it's alignment. It's the act of tuning your inner frequency to something larger, something unseen yet deeply present. Prayer and meditation, though ancient in practice, are among the most profound tools we have for shaping the quantum field.

## The Vibrational Power of Prayer

Prayer has often been thought of as a plea—a heartfelt request sent skyward in times of need. But what if prayer is more than asking? What if it's also aligning? In its truest form, prayer is a declaration of intention, spoken or unspoken, that aligns your energy with your desires. It's a way of focusing thought with clarity and purpose, sending it out like a beacon into the quantum field.

Think of the many forms prayer takes—silent contemplation, whispered words, even the repetitive rhythm of chanting. These actions create vibrations, literal and energetic, that resonate outward. Some studies have even shown that group prayer or meditation can have measurable effects on communities, reducing crime rates and increasing social harmony during synchronized efforts.

Group practices amplify the energy of intention, creating a collective resonance that extends beyond individual influence. Indigenous traditions, such as the Maori haka or the Sun Dance ceremonies of Native American tribes, emphasize the power of coming together to invoke healing, strength, and connection. These communal rituals mirror the findings of studies on group meditation, where the synchronized energy of participants has been shown to create measurable shifts in social dynamics, fostering peace and harmony on a wider scale

Is it coincidence? Or is it coherence, amplified by collective intention?

## Meditation: Listening to the Field

If prayer is speaking, meditation is listening. It is the stillness between the notes of a song, the pause that allows the universe to respond. In meditation, the mind becomes quiet, the chatter fades, and the static of daily life is replaced by clarity. This clarity is essential for aligning with the quantum field, as it clears the "noise" that can distort your intentions.

Meditation doesn't require complex rituals or hours of practice. It begins with a single breath. Close your eyes, inhale deeply, and focus on the rhythm of your breathing. In this state of presence, you may find insights, ideas, or even solutions to problems arising seemingly from nowhere. These moments are not random; they are the quantum field offering guidance, responding to the energy of your focus.

## Guided Exercise: The Breath of Alignment

Take a moment to pause. Sit comfortably and close your eyes. Breathe deeply in through your nose, holding for a count of three, then exhale slowly through your mouth. As you breathe, imagine each inhalation drawing in light and energy, and each exhalation releasing doubt or resistance. With each breath, visualize yourself tuning into a universal frequency, like a radio finding its signal. Feel the connection growing stronger, the alignment settling into place.

## The Science of Stillness

Modern neuroscience offers insights into why prayer and meditation are so powerful. When you meditate, your brainwaves shift from the busy beta state to the calm and focused alpha or even deeper theta states. These states are associated with creativity, intuition, and healing. Prayer, too, activates regions of the brain associated with empathy and connection, reinforcing the feeling that you are part of something greater.

On a quantum level, this shift in energy mirrors the principle of coherence, where scattered particles align into a unified whole. Your focused energy creates ripples in the quantum field, just as a calm mind sends clear signals into the universe.

## Real-World Resonance

Consider the story of a woman diagnosed with chronic pain who turned to meditation as a last resort. She began each day with 20 minutes of focused breathing and visualization, imagining her body healing itself. Over time, her pain lessened, and she experienced a profound sense of peace. Was it the power of her mind, the alignment of her intentions, or the quantum field responding to her clarity? Perhaps it was all three, working together in harmony.

Or think of a monk in a remote monastery, spending hours in silent prayer. His words are not shouted but whispered, yet they carry a resonance that can be felt far beyond the walls of his sanctuary. These moments remind us that the energy we cultivate within ourselves has the power to ripple outward, touching lives we may never meet.

### The Bridge Between Thought and Field

Prayer and meditation are not acts of passivity; they are acts of creation. They are the tools through which you tune your inner world to the frequency of the quantum field, amplifying the energy of your intentions. Whether through a whispered prayer or a silent meditation, these practices allow you to step into the flow of the universe, not as an observer but as a participant in its grand design.

So, the next time you sit quietly, whether in prayer, meditation, or simple reflection, remember this: you are not just connecting with the Divine; you are aligning with the infinite possibilities of the quantum field. And in that alignment, miracles are born.

# Visualization – Mentally Creating Desired Outcomes

Imagine standing in a quiet theater, the lights dimmed, and the stage empty. The curtains are drawn, but behind them, a story waits to unfold—a story written by you. This is the essence of visualization. It is the act of creating a mental picture so vivid and detailed that it feels as real as the world around you. In the quantum field, visualization is more than a daydream; it is a tool for shaping reality.

### The Quantum Blueprint

Visualization taps into one of the quantum field's most fascinating principles: the wave function. In quantum mechanics, particles exist in a state of potential, a kind of "cloud" of possibilities, until they are observed. The act of observing collapses these possibilities into a single, tangible reality. Visualization mirrors this process. When you imagine a desired outcome with clarity and focus, you are collapsing the "waves" of potential in your mind into a specific intention that resonates with the quantum field.

Think of your mind as an architect's table. Every thought is a blueprint, and every image you create becomes a foundation. For instance, when preparing for a job interview, visualization can help you embody confidence and clarity. Picture yourself walking into the room, speaking with assurance, and connecting authentically with your interviewers. By rehearsing this scene in your mind, you not only prepare yourself mentally but also align your energy with the desired outcome, increasing your likelihood of success.

The more detailed and precise your mental designs, the more likely they are to manifest in the physical world. This is not magic but resonance—your thoughts aligning with the vibrations of the universe to bring possibilities into being.

## From Dreams to Reality

Consider the story of a young inventor with a vision for renewable energy. Each night, he would sit in his room, sketching ideas and visualizing his designs powering homes around the world. He didn't just think about the end goal; he imagined the intricate details—how the machinery would look, the sound of it running, and the reactions of people using it. Over time, opportunities appeared: a chance meeting with a mentor, funding for his project, and eventually, a breakthrough invention. Was it luck? Or was it the power of focused visualization aligning him with the right people and circumstances?

Visualization is not simply wishful thinking. It requires an emotional connection to the image you create. When you visualize with feeling—excitement, gratitude, or confidence—you amplify the energy you send into the quantum field. It's the difference between watching a movie passively and stepping into the scene yourself. When you become emotionally engaged with your vision, the universe feels it too.

---

## Guided Exercise: Crafting Your Vision

Close your eyes and take a deep breath. Think of a goal or dream you hold close to your heart. Now, imagine it in as much detail as possible. What does it look like? What colors, shapes, or textures surround it? Next, engage your other senses. Can you hear sounds associated with this dream? Can you feel the emotions you would experience if it came true? Take your time, immersing yourself fully in the scene. When you open your eyes, carry that image with you as if it has already happened.

---

## The Science of Visualization

Modern studies have shown that visualization activates the same neural pathways as performing the actual activity. Athletes who mentally rehearse their movements, for example, show measurable improvements in their physical performance, even without additional practice. The brain does not fully distinguish between imagined and real experiences, which means your visualizations can train your mind—and even your body—for success.

On a quantum level, visualization aligns with the principle of resonance. By holding a clear mental image, you create a vibrational match between your thoughts and the potential outcomes in the field. This alignment increases the likelihood of those outcomes collapsing into reality.

## | *Real-World Transformations* |

One of the most famous examples of visualization in action comes from Olympic gold medalist **Michael Phelps**. Before every race, Phelps visualized every stroke, every turn, and even potential obstacles. He rehearsed not just the perfect swim but also how he would handle setbacks, ensuring his mind was prepared for any scenario. This mental practice, combined with physical training, made him one of the most successful athletes in history.

---

Another story involves a woman battling financial struggles. Each day, she spent time visualizing herself debt-free, imagining the weight lifting off her shoulders and the freedom she would feel. As she focused on this vision, she noticed opportunities arising—an unexpected promotion at work, a chance to reduce her expenses, and new ideas for side income. Over time, her visualization became her reality.

## Visualization as a Spiritual Practice

Visualization is more than a tool for achieving goals; it is a way of aligning with the divine. When you visualize, you are co-creating with the quantum field, stepping into the role of an artist shaping the masterpiece of your life. This practice invites you to trust in possibilities beyond what you can see, leaning into the unseen forces that guide and support you.

---

## Reflective Exercise: Trusting the Picture

As you go about your day, return to your vision. Hold it in your mind as if it has already come to pass. Notice how it changes the way you feel, the decisions you make, and the energy you project. Let this vision become a touchstone, reminding you that your thoughts have the power to shape your reality.

---

In visualization, we find a bridge between the seen and the unseen, the imagined and the real. It is the art of creating not just with hands or tools but with the mind itself, weaving dreams into existence one image at a time. And as we deepen this practice, we uncover another vital piece of the puzzle—faith. For even the clearest vision requires trust in the unseen mechanisms of the universe, a trust that we'll explore next.

# Faith in the Field — Trusting Unseen Mechanisms

Imagine planting a seed in the earth. You can't see it sprout right away, but you water it, nurture the soil, and trust that something miraculous is happening beneath the surface. This trust is what faith in the field looks like—a deep belief that unseen mechanisms are aligning to bring your intentions into reality. Faith isn't just hope; it's a quiet assurance that the universe is at work, even when there's no visible proof.

## The Unseen Forces of the Universe

Faith in the quantum field is about letting go of the need to control every detail and trusting the invisible threads that connect thought to outcome. In quantum physics, this idea is reflected in phenomena like quantum entanglement, where particles remain connected even when separated by vast distances. Their interactions, unseen yet undeniable, remind us that the universe operates in ways that often defy our understanding.

When you focus on a vision or goal, the field begins to respond, weaving together opportunities, connections, and synchronicities. These threads may not be immediately visible, but they are there, working in the background, aligning your external world with your internal intention.

### | *Real-Life Example: Journey of Harry Potter* |

Faith in the field was embodied by **J.K. Rowling** during her journey to publish the Harry Potter series. Rowling faced numerous rejections from publishers while living in financial difficulty, yet she held onto her belief in the story she had written. Despite every setback, she trusted that her work would one day find its audience. That faith carried her through the discouraging moments, and eventually, the field aligned. Her manuscript was accepted, and the Harry Potter series became one of the most successful literary franchises in history. This wasn't just persistence; it was trust in her vision and the unseen mechanisms guiding her path.

## The Role of Patience and Surrender

Faith requires patience, a willingness to let time unfold without rushing the process. Like the seed in the soil, some outcomes take time to germinate. This doesn't mean doing nothing—it means acting in alignment with your goals while releasing the need to force a specific timeline or outcome.

Surrender doesn't mean giving up; it means stepping back and allowing the quantum field to do its part. Think of it as a partnership: you set the intention and take inspired action, and the universe handles the rest.

## Guided Exercise: Trusting the Unseen

Find a quiet space and reflect on an area of your life where you feel stuck or uncertain. Close your eyes and take a few deep breaths. Visualize your desired outcome, then imagine placing it gently into the hands of the universe, like handing over a precious gift. Say to yourself, "I trust that everything is aligning perfectly, even if I can't see it yet." Feel the weight lift from your shoulders as you release the need to control every detail.

## Faith and Synchronicity

Have you ever experienced a moment of synchronicity—a chance meeting, an unexpected opportunity, or a perfectly timed event? These moments often feel like magic, but they are the quantum field's way of responding to your energy. Faith opens the door to synchronicities, which are moments of meaningful coincidence that align perfectly with your intentions. For example, you might be seeking a new job when a casual conversation with a stranger reveals an unexpected opportunity. These events are not random; they are the quantum field's way of signaling alignment between your internal state and external circumstances. When you cultivate faith, you create the mental and emotional space for these connections to emerge naturally.

Consider the story of Steve Jobs, who famously dropped out of college but trusted his intuition to guide him. He took a calligraphy class simply because it interested him, not knowing it would later inspire the groundbreaking fonts and design aesthetics of Apple computers. This is faith in action—following a path that feels right, even when the bigger picture isn't yet clear.

## The Balance Between Faith and Action

Faith doesn't mean sitting back and waiting for miracles to happen. It means taking inspired action while trusting the outcome. Think of faith as planting a garden: you must prepare the soil, sow the seeds, and water the plants, but you cannot force them to grow. By taking steps aligned with your intention and surrendering the rest, you create the conditions for the quantum field to work in harmony with your efforts.

Imagine driving a car at night. Your headlights only illuminate a small portion of the road, but you trust that the path ahead exists. Faith works the same way—it allows you to take one step at a time, confident that the field will reveal the next turn when the time is right.

## The Spiritual Depth of Faith

Faith is deeply spiritual. It connects you to the divine intelligence of the universe, reminding you that you are not alone in the process of creation. When you trust the field, you align yourself with something greater—a force that has been described in countless spiritual traditions as love, grace, or divine order.

In embracing faith, you learn to see the invisible, believe in the impossible, and trust that the universe is working tirelessly on your behalf. And as you hold onto this trust, you begin to notice the threads of connection weaving your dreams into reality, one unseen stitch at a time.

Faith is the final and perhaps most important piece of the manifestation puzzle. It is the bridge that carries you from intention to realization, reminding you that the quantum field is not just a concept but a partner in the creation of your life's masterpiece.

# Revisiting the Core Concepts and Insights

Picture a symphony, each instrument playing its part, the melodies weaving together seamlessly. That's the essence of **manifestation**—when your thoughts, intentions, and actions align, creating harmony with the quantum field. This chapter was a journey into that creative process, where the unseen and the tangible meet, and the universe becomes your collaborator.

**Intentionality** is the spark that ignites the process. A single thought, held with clarity and focus, is like planting a seed in fertile soil. It is the beginning of creation, where possibilities take root. The power of intention lies not in its complexity but in its precision. When your desires are clear, they resonate with the quantum field, setting into motion the unseen forces that shape your reality.

Then there is **prayer and meditation**, the tools that tune your inner frequency to the symphony of the universe. Prayer is the act of sending your desires into the field, like releasing a balloon into the sky, while meditation is the art of listening, of attuning yourself to the whispers of possibility that echo in the stillness. Together, they create a dialogue—a sacred exchange between you and the infinite.

**Visualization** is the canvas on which you paint your future. It transforms abstract dreams into vivid, living images. By engaging your senses and emotions, you collapse the potential into form, creating a vibrational blueprint that the universe can follow. Real stories of athletes, artists, and visionaries remind us that the power of visualization is not confined to imagination—it's a catalyst for action and alignment.

But none of these tools work without faith. **Faith** is the invisible bridge between intention and manifestation. It is trusting that the seed will sprout, even when the soil seems still. It is believing that the universe is working in your favor, even when the path ahead is unclear. Faith is the quiet assurance that synchronicities are not random but deliberate—a sign that the quantum field is responding to your energy.

When these elements come together, the result is nothing short of miraculous. Intentionality creates the vision, prayer and meditation align your energy, visualization paints the details, and faith ensures that the unseen mechanisms of the universe bring everything together. The quantum field doesn't just respond to what you want—it resonates with who you are, amplifying the energy you project into the world.

This process is not about controlling every outcome. It's about co-creating with a universe that is always listening, always responding. It's about understanding that your thoughts and emotions are not isolated—they ripple outward, influencing the field in ways you may never fully see. Every intention, every prayer, every moment of faith is a note in the symphony of creation.

As you reflect on the mechanics of manifestation, remember that this is more than a method—it's a way of living. It's an invitation to engage with life consciously, to see every thought as a choice, every emotion as a frequency, and every action as a step toward your highest potential. The quantum field is not separate from you; it is part of you, and you are part of it. Together, you create the music of your life.

And what happens when this symphony begins to flow effortlessly, when each note feels perfectly timed and every movement seems guided by an unseen hand? That is the state of flow, where you merge with the rhythm of the universe, and synchronicities become the signposts lighting your way.

As you learn to live in this alignment, you'll discover not just harmony but a deeper connection to the meaning behind it all.

# Chapter Six

# Flow States and Synchronicity – Living in Alignment

*"Flow is being completely involved in an activity for its own sake. The ego falls away. Time flies. Every action, movement, and thought follows inevitably from the previous one, like playing jazz."*

— Mihaly Csikszentmihalyi

Imagine walking a winding forest trail. The path unfolds effortlessly beneath your feet, each step perfectly placed. The rustle of leaves, the birdsong, and even the rhythm of your breath seem to move in harmony. Time dissolves, and the world feels alive with purpose. In this moment, you are not just existing—you are flowing, carried by an unseen current that connects you to everything around you. This is what it means to live in alignment with the quantum field.

This chapter explores how to live in effortless alignment with the universe by embracing flow states, recognizing synchronicities, and understanding the ripple effect of your actions. Flow is the experience of being so immersed in the present moment that you transcend effort and self-doubt, tapping into boundless energy and creativity. Synchronicity serves as the universe's way of showing you that you're on the right path, weaving together seemingly unrelated events into meaningful patterns. And through the ripple effect, we see how aligned actions resonate far beyond their origin, creating waves of impact in the lives of others.

# Flow State — Effortless Harmony with the Universe

## The State of Flow

Have you ever been so engrossed in an activity that the world around you seemed to fade away? Hours pass like minutes, and every movement or thought feels natural, almost automatic. This is the flow state—a profound sense of harmony where effort dissolves, and your actions feel guided by an invisible force. Athletes call it being "in the zone," while artists describe it as losing themselves in their craft.

In these moments, you are not just performing; you are resonating with the quantum field.

## The Science Behind Flow

Flow states occur when the brain enters a phase of 'transient hypofrontality,' where the prefrontal cortex temporarily quiets. This reduction in self-monitoring and critical thinking allows for heightened focus and creativity. Simultaneously, the brain releases a cocktail of neurochemicals—dopamine, endorphins, and norepinephrine—that enhance motivation, pleasure, and awareness. This neurobiological shift aligns your mental state with the energetic currents of the quantum field, allowing for seamless action and intuition.

But beyond the brain, flow has a deeper resonance with the universe. When you enter flow, you align your internal state with the rhythm of the quantum field. This alignment amplifies your creativity, intuition, and ability to make connections, as if the universe is working through you.

### | *Stories of Flow: The Surfer and the Wave* |

Picture a surfer riding a towering wave. In that moment, there's no time to calculate or plan. Every movement is instinctive, guided by the rhythm of the ocean. The surfer becomes one with the wave, moving in perfect harmony with its power. This is flow in its purest form—a state where human intention aligns effortlessly with the natural forces of the world.

---

## Accessing Flow in Daily Life

You don't need to be an athlete or artist to experience flow. It can happen during everyday activities, from writing an essay to cooking a meal. The key is to engage fully in the present moment, immersing yourself in the task at hand. Flow arises when your skills meet a challenge that stretches you without overwhelming you. It is a balance—a dance between effort and surrender.

## Reflective Exercise: Finding Your Flow

Take a moment to think about activities that make you lose track of time. What tasks or hobbies bring you joy and focus? Make a list of these activities and commit to doing one each week. When you engage in these moments, allow yourself to be fully present. Turn off distractions, focus on the process, and let yourself be carried by the rhythm of the task.

## Flow and the Quantum Field

In flow, you become a conduit for the universe's energy. Your actions, thoughts, and emotions align with the field, amplifying your ability to create and connect. This state is not just about productivity; it's about resonance. When you enter flow, you harmonize with the deeper currents of existence, allowing the universe to guide your movements.

## The Spiritual Depth of Flow

Many spiritual traditions describe states of flow without using the term. Whether it's a monk immersed in meditation, a dancer lost in movement, or a writer crafting words effortlessly, these moments reflect a deeper connection to the divine. In flow, the boundaries between self and universe blur, reminding us that we are part of something much greater.

In Hindu philosophy, this state aligns with the concept of *lila*—the divine play of creation. Flow is seen as a moment when the individual becomes a willing participant in this cosmic dance, surrendering to the movements of the universe. Similarly, Taoism describes wu wei, the art of effortless action, where harmony with the Tao allows life to unfold naturally and beautifully.

Flow is not a destination but a way of being—an invitation to step into alignment with the quantum field and let its currents carry you. As you navigate this state of harmony, you may begin to notice something remarkable: signs and patterns that seem to guide you, as if the universe itself is speaking. These are synchronicities, the whispers of alignment, and they are waiting to be discovered.

# Synchronicity — Meaningful Coincidences as Signs of Alignment

## The Language of the Universe

Imagine standing in a crowded room filled with the hum of indistinct chatter. Suddenly, you hear your name spoken across the room, and your attention sharpens, drawn instinctively to the sound. This is how synchronicity works—a signal rising above the noise, a moment so perfectly timed that it seems to carry a message just for you. These meaningful coincidences are the universe's way of speaking, guiding, and affirming that you are aligned with its flow.

## The Essence of Synchronicity

Synchronicities are not random events; they are patterns that emerge when your energy resonates with the quantum field. Carl Jung, the renowned psychologist, described synchronicity as "a meaningful coincidence," moments where the inner world of thoughts and emotions mirrors the outer world of events. These occurrences defy logic, yet they feel profoundly significant as if the universe is nudging you along the right path.

Think of synchronicity as the universe's way of winking—letting you know it sees your intentions, your efforts, and your alignment. It might appear as a chance encounter, a perfectly timed opportunity, or an unexpected insight that answers a question you've been pondering.

In the traditions of the Navajo people, the concept of hozho—a state of balance, beauty, and harmony—encapsulates this idea. Living in hozho means aligning one's thoughts, actions, and spirit with the natural order, creating a resonance that invites synchronicities. A hunter who intuitively senses where game will appear or a healer who discovers the exact herb needed for a remedy are examples of this alignment in action.

### | *Real-Life Synchronicity: The Wright Brothers* |

Consider the story of the Wright brothers, who dreamed of human flight. As they worked tirelessly on their designs, a series of seemingly chance events occurred—conversations with key individuals, discoveries of materials, and breakthroughs in understanding aerodynamics. Each step seemed improbably aligned as if the universe itself wanted to see humanity take to the skies. Their story reflects how synchronicities often arise when passion, focus, and intention converge with the quantum field.

## Recognizing Synchronicity

Synchronicities often appear as subtle moments, easily dismissed if you're not paying attention. Perhaps you've experienced thinking of an old friend, only to have them call you out of the blue. Or you've been seeking a solution to a problem, only to stumble across the perfect resource at just the right time. These moments feel like serendipity, but they are more than luck—they are signs of alignment.

To invite more synchronicities into your life, start by setting clear intentions. For example, if you're seeking guidance, write down a specific question or goal and reflect on it daily. Practice mindfulness to attune yourself to subtle cues in your environment—songs on the radio, snippets of conversation, or recurring symbols.

Keep a synchronicity journal to track these moments, noting any patterns or insights that emerge over time.

---

## Guided Exercise: Tracking Your Synchronicities

Take a moment to reflect on your day or week. Have there been any unusual coincidences or moments that felt perfectly timed? Write them down in a journal, noting how they made you feel and what thoughts or questions you were holding at the time. Over time, patterns may emerge, revealing how the universe communicates with you.

---

## The Science of Patterns

While synchronicity feels magical, it also has roots in how our brains and the quantum field interact. The brain is wired to recognize patterns, and when your thoughts and emotions are focused on a particular goal, you become more attuned to opportunities that align with that focus. On a quantum level, your energy resonates outward, creating connections that draw these opportunities into your awareness.

### | *Stories of Synchronicity* |

One striking example of synchronicity comes from the world of music. Paul McCartney famously shared that the melody for "Yesterday," one of The Beatles' greatest hits, came to him in a dream. Unsure of its origin, he played the tune for others, convinced he must have subconsciously borrowed it. When no one recognized it, he realized the melody was original—a gift seemingly delivered through the alignment of his creative focus and the quantum field.

---

## The Spiritual Depth of Synchronicity

In spiritual traditions, synchronicity is often seen as divine guidance. Whether it's an ancient sage interpreting omens or a modern seeker noticing angel numbers, these moments serve as reminders of a deeper connection between the individual and the universe. Synchronicity invites you to trust the journey, even when the destination is unclear, and to believe that the universe is always conspiring in your favor.

## Living in Tune with Synchronicity

The more you align with the flow of the quantum field, the more frequently synchronicities will appear. These moments are like breadcrumbs on the trail, guiding you toward your goals and affirming that you are on the right path. By cultivating awareness and gratitude for these signs, you strengthen your connection to the field, inviting even more meaningful coincidences into your life.

Synchronicity reminds us that we are not separate from the universe but deeply connected to its rhythms. As you tune into these moments of alignment, you may begin to see how the ripples of your actions extend far beyond yourself, touching lives and shaping the world in ways you never imagined.

# Ripple Effect – The Far-Reaching Impact of Aligned Actions

## The Energy You Send Out

Drop a single stone into a calm lake, and the ripples expand outward, touching the shorelines you cannot see. In much the same way, your thoughts, intentions, and actions send waves of energy into the quantum field, influencing not just your life but the lives of others. This interconnected nature of existence means that when you align yourself with higher vibrations—love, kindness, purpose—you are not just shaping your reality. You are contributing to a larger symphony that resonates far beyond your immediate experience.

## The Science of Influence

The ripple effect is not merely a poetic idea; it has roots in both psychology and quantum physics. Studies in social networks show how emotions and behaviors spread like wildfire. A single act of kindness can inspire a chain of similar actions, creating waves of positivity that touch countless lives. Similarly, on a quantum level, energy and information are not confined to one space but can influence far-reaching outcomes. Your aligned actions resonate with the field, amplifying their impact in ways you may never fully witness.

### | *Real-Life Ripple: Greta Thunberg* |

Consider **Greta Thunberg**, a teenager who began her journey with a solitary school strike for climate awareness. Her individual action, aligned with her unwavering intention to make a difference, resonated globally. What started as one voice in her local community became a worldwide movement, inspiring millions to rethink their relationship with the planet. Greta's story demonstrates how a single, purposeful act can send ripples through the quantum field, galvanizing collective action on an unimaginable scale.

## Your Impact on Relationships

Alignment is not just about grand gestures; it's about the energy you bring into everyday interactions. When you approach others with compassion and authenticity, you set the tone for deeper connections. Have you ever noticed how a genuine smile can brighten someone's day or how a kind word can shift the mood of an entire room? These seemingly small acts carry energy that ripples outward, influencing not only the immediate moment but also the interactions that follow.

## Guided Reflection: Tracing Your Ripples

Think back to a time when someone's kindness or encouragement made a lasting impact on you. What ripple did that action create in your life? Now, consider your own actions—how have your words or deeds influenced others? Take a moment to visualize the ripples of energy you are sending out, and ask yourself: Are they aligned with the reality I wish to create?

## The Legacy of Aligned Actions

Your influence is not limited to the present moment. Aligned actions have the power to create a legacy, shaping the lives of people you may never meet. Think of the ripple effect of historical figures whose intentions resonated long after they were gone. Martin Luther King Jr.'s vision of equality continues to inspire movements worldwide, reminding us that alignment with purpose has enduring power.

## The Quantum Connection

On a quantum level, the ripple effect speaks to the interconnected nature of the universe. Just as particles influence one another across great distances, your energy interacts with the field, creating patterns that extend far beyond your awareness. This is not limited to physical actions; your thoughts and intentions, too, are waves in the field, influencing outcomes in subtle and profound ways.

### | *Story of a Ripple: One Teacher's Influence* |

A high school teacher once committed to seeing the potential in every student, regardless of their circumstances. Her encouragement inspired one struggling student to believe in himself, leading him to pursue a college education. That student went on to become a successful entrepreneur, creating jobs and opportunities for others in his community. This chain of influence, initiated by one teacher's aligned intention, continues to ripple outward, touching lives far removed from the original act.

---

## Expanding the Ripple Effect

When your actions resonate with the quantum field, their impact grows exponentially. By aligning with higher values—love, gratitude, service—you amplify the reach of your influence. The ripple effect reminds us that no action is too small and no intention too insignificant. Every wave you send into the field contributes to the greater harmony of existence.

The ripples you create are not confined to your immediate circle; they spread across time and space, interweaving with the energy of others to shape the world we share. And when these ripples align with the universe's flow, they open the door to something extraordinary—living in harmony with synchronicities and flow, a state where life feels almost magical.

## Call-to-Action

Challenge yourself to create a positive ripple today. Perform one act of kindness—offer a compliment, help a neighbor, or donate to a cause. Then, reflect on how that action might influence others. Imagine the person you helped paying it forward, spreading positivity like ripples on a pond. By consciously creating ripples, you contribute to the collective energy of harmony and alignment.

## Revisiting the Core Concepts and Insights

Life, when lived in **alignment**, becomes less of a struggle and more of a dance. In this chapter, we explored the profound simplicity of living in flow with the universe—a state where effort dissolves into ease and the boundaries between self and the infinite blur. Flow isn't just a psychological phenomenon; it's a spiritual experience, a moment when you become a conduit for the energy of creation. It is in this state that life feels intuitive, where solutions appear before problems have fully formed and where each step feels guided by an unseen hand.

**Synchronicities**, the universe's whispers, show us the signs that we're walking the right path. They're not accidents or random occurrences; they are markers of alignment. These moments, whether small or life-altering, remind us that we are part of a larger, interconnected whole. They are the universe saying, "Yes, you are exactly where you need to be."

But alignment is not just about individual experiences—it **ripples** outward, touching lives we may never meet. The choices you make, the energy you bring, and the intentions you set send waves through the quantum field. Like a stone dropped into still water, your actions create patterns, influencing not only your own reality but the realities of others. These ripples remind us that alignment is not a solitary act; it is a contribution to the collective symphony of existence.

Living in **flow** with the quantum field invites us to trust in the unseen, to recognize that our efforts and intentions are always met with a response, even if it's not immediately visible. It calls us to embrace synchronicity as guidance and to see our every action as part of a greater ripple effect. To live this way is to live with purpose, to see the extraordinary in the ordinary, and to walk each day with a quiet confidence that the universe is working alongside you.

As we reflect on the interconnectedness of flow, synchronicity, and the ripple effect, we're reminded that alignment is not an endpoint but a practice—a way of being. It's a choice to step into harmony with the rhythms of the quantum field, to let go of resistance, and to allow life to unfold in its natural grace. The beauty of this alignment lies in its simplicity: when you trust the flow, the flow begins to trust you.

And yet, even as we strive for alignment, barriers arise—fear, doubt, resistance. These forces challenge us, pulling us out of flow and into stagnation. But every obstacle holds a lesson, a chance to grow stronger in our connection to the quantum field.

...

As we step forward, we'll explore how to navigate the challenges that pull us out of alignment—fear, doubt, and resistance. These forces, though daunting, hold the keys to unlocking even greater flow, synchronicity, and co-creation.

By embracing them, we move closer to living fully in harmony with the quantum field

# Chapter Seven

# Breaking Barriers to Co-Creation

*"When you change the way you look at things,
the things you look at change."*

\- Wayne Dyer

Consider a bird perched at the edge of a branch, wings twitching with uncertainty. The air, vast and open, holds the promise of freedom, yet the bird hesitates, gripped by an unseen tether—fear. We are much like that bird, holding the potential to soar into alignment with the quantum field but often restrained by the invisible weights of doubt, ego, and limiting beliefs. These barriers may not be physical, but they are real, shaping our experiences and keeping us from stepping fully into the flow of co-creation.

This chapter delves into the common obstacles that stand between us and alignment with the quantum field. Fear and doubt cloud our ability to trust the unseen mechanisms at work, while ego and resistance pull us into cycles of control and separation. Limiting beliefs, often buried deep in our subconscious, keep us tethered to old patterns, preventing us from seeing the vast possibilities available to us. By recognizing and addressing these barriers, we can clear the path to co-creation, allowing our intentions to resonate freely with the energy of the universe.

## Fear and Doubt – Emotional Barriers to Alignment

### The Weight of Fear

Fear has a way of gripping the mind, pulling focus from possibility to peril. It whispers of what might go wrong, magnifying every potential misstep until even the simplest actions feel paralyzing. Doubt, its quiet accomplice, erodes trust in both the self and the universe, leaving us stranded in a fog of indecision. These emotions are not just fleeting feelings; they are barriers that sever our connection to the quantum field.

Fear stems from a survival mechanism deeply embedded in our biology. It served our ancestors well, keeping them alert to danger. But in today's world, fear often latches onto intangible threats—failure, rejection, and the unknown. It narrows our focus, trapping us in patterns of self-preservation that block creativity, intuition, and connection.

## Doubt and the Erosion of Trust

Doubt works subtly, undermining faith in unseen mechanisms. It tells us that our intentions are too lofty, our goals unattainable, our efforts futile. When doubt takes hold, it weakens our ability to resonate with the quantum field, scattering the energy needed to manifest our desires. Trust—the cornerstone of alignment—becomes shaky, and without trust, co-creation falters.

### | *Real-Life Story: Nelson Mandela's Resolve* |

Nelson Mandela spent 27 years in prison, much of that time in solitary confinement. He could have succumbed to fear and doubt, overwhelmed by the impossibility of his situation. Instead, he nurtured an unwavering vision of equality and reconciliation, trusting that even in isolation, his actions and intentions were resonating beyond the walls of his cell. His release and subsequent leadership were not just political victories—they were triumphs of faith over fear, a reminder that trust in a greater purpose can dissolve even the most formidable barriers.

## The Energy of Fear in the Quantum Field

Fear and doubt are not merely emotions; they are vibrations, and like all vibrations, they interact with the quantum field. When you dwell in fear, your energy resonates with limitation and separation, drawing experiences that mirror these states. Conversely, when you choose courage and trust, you align with expansive possibilities, inviting the universe to respond in kind.

## Guided Reflection: Facing Your Fear

Take a quiet moment to identify a fear or doubt that has been holding you back. Visualize it as a shadowy shape in your mind's eye. Now, picture a warm light emanating from your heart, gradually dissolving the shadow. As the fear fades, repeat silently: "I release this fear and trust in the guidance of the universe."

As the tension eases, reflect on a moment when you trusted despite uncertainty. How did that trust guide you to a positive outcome? Let this memory serve as proof that trust is a bridge to possibility.

---

## Reframing Fear as a Teacher

Fear is not inherently bad; it can be a powerful teacher, pointing to areas where growth is needed. Instead of resisting fear, ask what it's trying to show you. Often, fear highlights limiting beliefs or unresolved emotions that need to be addressed before you can move forward. By facing fear with curiosity instead of avoidance, you transform it from a barrier into a bridge.

## Trust as the Antidote

The antidote to fear and doubt is trust—not blind faith, but a deep-seated confidence in the interplay between your intentions and the quantum field. Trust allows you to take risks, to step forward even when the path is unclear. It frees you from the need to control every outcome, creating space for synchronicity and flow to enter.

Fear and doubt may be inevitable parts of the human experience, but they do not have to define it. By recognizing these emotions for what they are—signals, not sentences—you regain the power to align with the field. And as trust grows, you'll find that the energy of resistance begins to dissolve, making way for something far greater: the freedom to co-create without limits.

# Ego and Resistance – Internal Conflicts That Hinder Connection

## The Illusion of Control

In many wisdom traditions, surrender is seen not as weakness but as an act of divine alignment—a moment when the individual steps aside to let the greater order unfold. Ego resists this truth, clinging to control as if it alone can shape the tides of destiny. Yet this very need to dominate—to force outcomes, to prove ourselves—often blocks the flow of creation. The ego thrives on separation: me versus them, my success versus their failure. It's a voice that shouts when silence is needed, a force that resists the gentle whispers of the universe.

Resistance, its close ally, digs in when life nudges us toward growth. It clings to comfort, to familiarity, to the safety of the known. Together, ego and resistance create barriers, walls that keep us from connecting to the quantum field, from flowing with its rhythms. These walls may feel protective, but they are prisons of our own making.

## | *A Lesson in Letting Go: Muhammad Ali* |

**Muhammad Ali's** story isn't just about boxing; it's about surrendering ego to align with purpose. Stripped of his title for refusing the Vietnam draft, Ali faced public scorn and the loss of his livelihood. He could have fought back in anger, let his ego demand retribution. Instead, he stood firm in his principles, resisting not the consequences but the temptation to betray his values. Ali's alignment with his higher purpose transcended resistance, making him not just a champion in the ring but a symbol of conviction and courage.

---

## The Tug of War Within

Resistance often shows up in subtle ways—a procrastinated project, a hesitation to take the leap, an inner voice whispering, Not yet. Not good enough. These are not external forces; they are reflections of internal conflict. Ego fears vulnerability and failure, so it resists change, even when that change leads to growth.

This tug of war within keeps us stuck. The more we resist, the harder the struggle becomes, like trying to row upstream against a powerful current. Yet the moment we let go, the current carries us, often in directions we couldn't have planned but desperately needed.

## The Quantum Field and Surrender

On a quantum level, ego and resistance create discord. Where flow requires alignment and openness, ego demands control, disrupting the harmony needed for co-creation. Resistance blocks the signals you send to the field, scattering your intentions. Surrender, on the other hand, aligns your energy with the universe, allowing it to work through you.

Surrender is not passive. It's an active choice to release the need to control every variable and trust the field's response. It's saying, I will show up with intention, but I will not cling to the outcome. This trust invites synchronicity, where the field's wisdom complements your effort.

---

## Guided Reflection: Releasing Resistance

Close your eyes and think of a situation where you've been holding tight to control. Visualize your grip loosening, your hands opening as if releasing a bird into the sky. Feel the relief of surrender, the weight lifting from your shoulders. Say to yourself, I release resistance and allow life to flow through me.

As you release resistance, imagine yourself as a leaf carried by a stream, flowing effortlessly with the current. This is wu wei, the Taoist art of harmonious action, where surrender leads to ease and purpose.Let that sense of openness guide your next steps.

---

## Resistance Transformed

Resistance is not the enemy; it's a signal. It shows us where we're afraid to step forward, where old wounds or beliefs hold us back. By listening to resistance, you can uncover what needs healing and what needs to be released. When resistance becomes a teacher instead of an obstacle, it loses its power to confine.

## Ego as a Servant, Not a Master

The ego's voice will always be there, but it doesn't have to lead the conversation. When tempered with humility and aligned with purpose, ego can be a tool rather than a barrier. It can drive ambition and courage without disconnecting you from the flow of the field. The key is to let purpose guide the ego, not the other way around.

Ali's story, like countless others, reminds us that true power lies in surrender, not domination. The quantum field doesn't respond to the loudest voice; it responds to the clearest signal. And when ego quiets, and resistance softens, that signal becomes strong, inviting alignment, growth, and co-creation.

As we dissolve these barriers within, another layer of self-discovery comes into focus—our beliefs, the unseen frameworks that shape our reality. And sometimes, the greatest shifts come not from doing more but from rethinking what we hold to be true.

# Limiting Beliefs – Reframing Thought Patterns to Unlock Potential

## The Invisible Cage

Limiting beliefs are like invisible walls. You can't always see them, but you can feel their presence, holding you back from stepping into your full potential. These beliefs are not truths; they are stories we've absorbed—often without question—from our past, from society, or from our own fears. They whisper, You're not smart enough, not strong enough, not worthy. And the worst part? They sound so convincing that we rarely stop to challenge them.

These beliefs operate in the background, shaping the way we see ourselves, others, and the world. They filter possibilities, dismissing opportunities before we can even recognize them. Left unchecked, they form the foundation of our decisions, quietly dictating what we believe is possible.

## The Quantum Impact of Belief

Imagine your beliefs as the lens of a projector. A cloudy lens distorts the image, while a clear lens allows the full vibrancy of the picture to shine through. The quantum field reflects back the clarity—or distortion—of your beliefs. It amplifies whatever signal you send.

If your inner narrative is filled with scarcity, doubt, or impossibility, the field mirrors that back. But when your beliefs align with abundance, confidence, and potential, the field responds with opportunities and synchronicities that match that energy.

Beliefs are powerful because they create resonance. A belief held deeply enough vibrates through your actions, choices, and even the energy you project. It's not just what you say or do—it's what you believe that shapes your reality.

### | *Real-Life Transformation: The 4-Minute Mile* |

For decades, it was believed that running a mile in under four minutes was impossible. Medical experts warned that attempting such a feat could be fatal. This belief held athletes back—not because their bodies couldn't achieve it, but because their minds had already decided it was impossible.

In 1954, **Roger Bannister** shattered that belief. Running the mile in three minutes and 59.4 seconds, he didn't just break a record—he broke a collective limiting belief. Within a year, multiple athletes accomplished the same feat, proving that the barrier had never been physical. It was mental. Bannister's story is a powerful reminder of how reframing beliefs can open the door to new possibilities.

## Identifying Limiting Beliefs

The first step in overcoming limiting beliefs is recognizing them. These beliefs often disguise themselves as practical concerns or "truths" about the way the world works. A limiting belief might sound like:

> *I'm too old to start something new.*

> *I'll never be as successful as they are.*

> *I'm not creative enough to solve this problem.*

These statements feel like facts, but they are merely perceptions—perceptions that can be challenged and changed.

## Guided Reflection: Naming Your Beliefs

Take a moment to think about a goal or dream that feels out of reach. Write down the thoughts that arise when you imagine pursuing it. Are they encouraging or dismissive? If they lean toward doubt or limitation, ask yourself: "Where did this belief come from? Is it rooted in truth, or is it a story I've been telling myself?" Often, simply identifying a limiting belief is enough to weaken its hold.

## Reframing Beliefs

Reframing a belief begins with awareness but is strengthened through repetition and action. Replace limiting beliefs with empowering ones:

> Instead of, *I'm too old,* try, *It's never too late to grow and learn.*

> Instead of, *I'm not creative enough,* say, *Creativity grows with practice, and I am open to exploring it.*

These new beliefs may feel foreign at first, but over time, they create new neural pathways, rewiring your brain to align with possibility rather than limitation.

## The Role of Self-Talk

Your internal dialogue is a direct reflection of your beliefs. If your self-talk is harsh or dismissive, it reinforces limitation. But when your inner voice becomes kind, encouraging, and confident, it shifts the energy you project into the field. This shift doesn't happen overnight, but with consistent effort, you can create a self-dialogue that supports your highest potential.

## The Ripple Effect of Reframing

Changing your beliefs doesn't just impact your life—it influences those around you. When you break free from limitations, you inspire others to question their own. Consider how Roger Bannister's achievement didn't just open doors for him; it redefined what was possible for every runner who followed. In the same way, your journey to overcome limiting beliefs can create ripples of possibility for others.

## The Spiritual Perspective on Beliefs

From a spiritual lens, limiting beliefs separate us from the divine potential within us. They disconnect us from the truth that we are co-creators with the universe, capable of manifesting extraordinary outcomes. By letting go of these mental barriers, we align more fully with the quantum field and the Creator's design for growth, expansion, and joy.

### | *Real-Life Transformation: Astronaut Jessica Watkins* |

In 2021, **Jessica Watkins** became NASA's first Black female astronaut to join a long-duration spaceflight crew. Despite societal and systemic barriers, her belief in her potential, paired with relentless effort, paved the way for a historic accomplishment. Her story reminds us that reframing limiting beliefs is not just personal—it can redefine collective possibilities.

## Moving Beyond the Invisible Cage

Limiting beliefs are not permanent. They are learned, and what is learned can be unlearned. Each time you challenge a belief, each time you take a step in faith, you weaken the cage that once confined you. And as those walls crumble, the field begins to respond with opportunities you once thought impossible.

The beauty of reframing beliefs is that it doesn't just change your perspective—it changes your reality. As the invisible cage disappears, you step into a life that feels boundless, guided not by fear or doubt but by trust in the infinite possibilities of the quantum field.

## Revisiting the Core Concepts and Insights

Life offers a choice: remain bound by invisible barriers or step into the freedom of alignment. **Fear and doubt** whisper limitations, pulling focus from possibilities to dangers, yet they are signals more than sentences. When met with trust and courage, these emotions lose their grip, and the quantum field responds in kind. Every time you move beyond fear, you send a ripple of bravery into the universe, inviting opportunities to meet you halfway.

**Ego and resistance** often disguise themselves as protectors, but they weigh us down, keeping us locked in patterns of control and separation. True freedom comes not from clinging but from releasing, from trusting the flow rather than fighting it. The universe moves with rhythm and purpose, but it requires our openness to join the dance. Surrender is not weakness; it is the strength to let go of what no longer serves and embrace what is meant to be.

**Limiting beliefs** act as unseen anchors, keeping us tethered to outdated versions of ourselves. These beliefs are not truths but inherited scripts, often absorbed without question. When they are challenged, rewritten, and reframed, they cease to confine us. The stories we tell ourselves shape the realities we live, and by changing the narrative, we change the field of possibilities. Every belief reimagined is a door opened to a new version of life.

The energy you project—whether rooted in fear or trust, resistance or surrender, limitation or potential—ripples far beyond you. Your thoughts, intentions, and actions resonate with the quantum field, shaping not only your path but the paths of others. The impact of your alignment extends outward, creating waves of influence that connect you to the greater whole.

These barriers—fear, ego, and limiting beliefs—are not walls but invitations. They challenge you to grow, to expand your understanding of yourself and the universe, and to align more deeply with the energy of creation. Each obstacle overcome is a step closer to co-creation, where your desires harmonize with the divine order, and life unfolds with purpose and grace.

...

The mind is a powerful architect, capable of shaping the reality it perceives. When fear, ego, and limiting beliefs dissolve, they reveal a vast potential waiting to be claimed. Yet, what if the act of belief itself held the key to unlocking this potential? There is a phenomenon—rooted in both science and faith—that shows how the expectations of the mind can transform the body, heal the spirit, and bend reality. It is a reminder that the connection between belief and manifestation is not only profound but measurable, offering a glimpse into the intricate relationship between thought and creation.

As you dismantle the barriers of fear, ego, and limiting beliefs, you begin to access the full power of co-creation. But what if belief itself holds an even greater potential—a force that can heal, transform, and reshape reality at its very core?

From here, we will explore the extraordinary connection between belief and manifestation, uncovering how the mind's expectations influence the quantum field and the very fabric of existence.

# Chapter Eight

# The Placebo Effect and the Power of Belief

*"You are the placebo. Your thoughts can make you sick, and your thoughts can make you well."*

– Dr. Joe Dispenza

Picture this: a man is handed a sugar pill and told it will cure his chronic headaches. Days later, the pain that plagued him for years vanishes. What changed? Not the chemistry of the pill—it was just sugar—but the chemistry of his mind. This is the placebo effect, a phenomenon that defies logic and underscores one undeniable truth: belief has the power to shape reality.

This chapter explores the profound influence of belief and expectation on the body, mind, and quantum field. Through the lens of the placebo effect, we uncover how the mind's power extends far beyond what science once thought possible. Aligning belief systems with desired outcomes is not a passive act but a deliberate alignment of thought and intention that unlocks the potential of co-creation. At the heart of it all lies faith—not blind faith, but a knowing trust in the connection between what we hold in our minds and what manifests in our lives.

## The Scientific Basis of the Placebo Effect

### The Mind as a Healer

What if the greatest pharmacy didn't require a prescription but resided within the brain? The placebo effect offers us a glimpse into this remarkable possibility. Defined as the body's ability to heal or improve simply because the mind believes in a treatment, the placebo effect is not a fluke; it is proof that belief can override biology. From reducing pain to alleviating symptoms of chronic illness, the placebo effect has baffled and intrigued researchers for decades.

## The Power of Perception

The placebo effect reveals that healing begins not in the treatment itself but in the mind's belief in its efficacy. When the brain anticipates positive results, it releases powerful neurochemicals such as endorphins and dopamine, which simulate the effects of actual medical interventions. This phenomenon is so impactful that placebo treatments have significantly alleviated symptoms of depression, irritable bowel syndrome, and even chronic pain. It underscores a remarkable truth: the mind holds the blueprint for initiating the body's healing processes.

### | *Scientific Studies That Prove the Effect* |

In one groundbreaking study, researchers investigated the placebo effect in knee surgeries for patients with osteoarthritis. Participants were divided into three groups: one received actual arthroscopic debridement (removal of damaged cartilage), another underwent arthroscopic lavage (flushing of the joint), and the third group received a sham surgery where only skin incisions were made, but no actual procedure was performed.

The sham surgery group reported pain relief and improved mobility comparable to the groups that underwent real surgeries. The results suggested that the belief in the surgery's efficacy, rather than the procedure itself, contributed significantly to the outcomes.

Another study explored the placebo effect in patients with Parkinson's disease, a neurological disorder characterized by dopamine deficiency. Participants were told they were receiving an advanced treatment, but instead, they were administered a placebo. Brain imaging and biochemical tests revealed that placebo administration triggered dopamine release in the brain, mimicking the effects of actual medication.

The study demonstrated that the mere belief in treatment could produce physiological changes in the brain, highlighting the profound influence of expectation on biological processes.

———————

## The Quantum Field Connection

The placebo effect extends beyond biological processes and into the energetic realm of the quantum field. When an individual deeply believes in the possibility of healing, their energy aligns with this intention, creating a coherent signal that interacts with the quantum field. This resonance not only enhances the body's natural healing mechanisms but also attracts opportunities, resources, and synchronicities that support the healing process. This interplay suggests that belief isn't confined to the body—it's a force that reverberates through the very fabric of reality.

## The Limitations of Skepticism

Skepticism, while healthy in moderation, can undermine the placebo effect. If a person does not believe in the possibility of healing, their brain does not release the same chemical signals. This demonstrates that belief is not just a passive thought but an active force that shapes outcomes. The mind must be willing to trust and to suspend doubt long enough for the field to respond.

---

### Guided Reflection: Exploring Your Beliefs About Healing

Take a moment to consider how your beliefs about health and healing might be influencing your body. Do you trust in your ability to recover, or do doubt and fear dominate your thoughts? Write down one belief about your health that feels limiting. Then, reframe it into an empowering statement, such as, My body has an innate ability to heal. Repeat this statement daily, allowing it to reshape your mental and physical energy.

---

## A Lesson in Possibility

The placebo effect teaches us that belief is not a trivial force—it is the foundation of how we interact with the world. It reminds us that our thoughts are not confined to our minds; they ripple outward, influencing both our internal biology and the external reality we experience. And as we deepen our understanding of this phenomenon, we begin to see how aligning belief systems can transform not just health but every aspect of life.

# Aligning Belief Systems with Desired Outcomes

## The Power of a Focused Mind

The mind is a compass, constantly setting the direction of our lives. When your beliefs are scattered, pulling in conflicting directions, the journey feels slow and aimless. But when your beliefs align with a clear goal, the path becomes smoother and more purposeful. Aligning belief systems with desired outcomes is not just a mental exercise—it's an energetic recalibration that resonates with the quantum field, inviting opportunities and synchronicities to flow.

## Beliefs as Filters

Every experience you have is filtered through the lens of your beliefs. If you believe the world is full of scarcity, you'll see lack wherever you look. If you believe abundance is possible, opportunities seem to appear as if by magic. This isn't coincidence; it's the result of your mind priming itself to notice what aligns with your dominant thought patterns. The quantum field responds to these patterns, amplifying the energy you project.

## The Challenge of Limiting Beliefs

Misaligned or limiting beliefs act like static on a radio. They distort the signal you send to the universe, weakening your ability to connect with the quantum field. Beliefs such as I'm not good enough or success isn't meant for people like me create resistance, blocking the flow of energy needed to manifest desired outcomes. Identifying and replacing these beliefs is the first step toward alignment.

## Rewriting the Narrative

Transforming your belief system begins with cultivating awareness. Notice the internal dialogue that emerges during moments of doubt or challenge. Are these narratives empowering, or do they reinforce limitation? Once you identify a limiting belief, dissect its origins. Ask: Is this belief rooted in truth, or is it a perspective I've adopted unconsciously? Replace these limiting perspectives with empowering affirmations that align with your goals.

For example, if you find yourself thinking, *I'll never reach that goal*, reframe it to, *I am continuously learning, evolving, and moving closer to my aspirations.* This simple shift creates a profound ripple effect, gradually rewiring your mindset and reshaping the energy you project into the quantum field.

## | *Real-Life Example: Serena Williams* |

**Serena Williams** didn't become one of the greatest athletes in history by accident. Throughout her career, she has spoken about the role of belief in her success. Even in the face of injury or doubt, she maintained an unwavering belief in her ability to win. Her thoughts, words, and actions aligned with her vision of excellence, creating a powerful resonance with the outcomes she desired. Serena's story is a testament to how aligning belief systems can fuel extraordinary achievements.

## Belief and the Quantum Field

When you align your beliefs with your goals, you create coherence in your energy field. This alignment strengthens the signal you send into the quantum field, amplifying your ability to manifest. It's not about wishful thinking; it's about creating resonance between your inner state and the reality you want to experience. The field responds to clarity, and aligned beliefs provide that clarity.

## The Role of Emotional Energy

The potency of a belief is magnified when infused with emotion. A thought such as *I am successful* remains hollow without an emotional connection to reinforce it. However, when this belief is paired with a deep sense of joy, gratitude, and confidence, it transforms into a powerful magnetic force. Emotional energy serves as the driving current, propelling your intentions into the quantum field and transforming abstract thoughts into tangible realities.

## Exercise: The Visualization of Alignment

Take a quiet moment to focus on a goal you've been working toward. Close your eyes and picture the outcome as vividly as you can. What does it feel like to achieve it? Allow the emotions of success—joy, pride, gratitude—to fill you. Hold onto these feelings as you repeat a belief aligned with your goal, such as I am capable of creating this reality. This practice strengthens the resonance of your belief, aligning your energy with your desired outcome.

## The Ripple Effect of Belief Alignment

When your beliefs align with your goals, the impact doesn't stop with you. Your energy influences those around you, creating a ripple effect that inspires and uplifts. Think of a leader whose unwavering belief in a vision motivates an entire team to achieve the impossible. Alignment isn't just personal; it's contagious.

### Faith as a Foundation

At the heart of aligning belief systems is faith—not blind faith, but trust in the connection between your thoughts, energy, and the quantum field. Faith bridges the gap between what you believe and what becomes reality. It's the thread that holds the process together, encouraging you to keep going even when evidence of success isn't immediately visible.

When beliefs align with outcomes, the field responds. Opportunities appear challenges transform into stepping stones, and life begins to feel less like a battle and more like a partnership with the universe. This alignment creates a foundation for the next step in co-creation: understanding the deeper role of faith in shaping the world around us.

## The Role of Faith in Shaping Reality

### Faith as the Bridge

Faith is the quiet power that transforms possibility into reality. It's not merely wishful thinking or blind optimism—it is a knowing faith works in harmony with the quantum field, orchestrating outcomes that align with the energy you project. Unlike doubt, which scatters energy and weakens intention, faith creates focus and coherence. It acts as a stabilizing force, allowing you to move forward with clarity even when the path ahead seems unclear. Faith, in essence, is the bridge between your intention and the unseen forces that bring it to life.

### The Energy of Faith

Faith is more than a belief—it's a vibration, a frequency that resonates with possibility. When paired with intention, faith amplifies your connection to the quantum field, strengthening the signals you send. This resonance creates coherence, making your thoughts and actions more powerful and focused. Without faith, doubt creeps in, scattering energy and disrupting alignment.

Faith is not about blind optimism or ignoring reality; it's about trusting in the unseen mechanisms that guide the interplay between thought and creation. It is the quiet knowing that the universe is working alongside you, even when circumstances suggest otherwise.

## The Energy of Trust

When you act with faith, you send a signal into the quantum field that says, I believe in this possibility, and I am ready to receive it. This energy is magnetic, drawing opportunities and resources toward you. Faith doesn't demand immediate evidence; it thrives in the unseen, trusting that the field is responding even when outcomes have yet to materialize. This trust creates alignment, making your intentions resonate with the frequencies of creation.

### | *Real-Life Faith: Martin Luther King Jr.* |

Martin Luther King Jr. embodied the power of faith in action. His vision of equality was not yet visible in the world he lived in, but he spoke and acted as though it was inevitable. His famous words, "I have a dream," were not just a declaration—they were an act of faith. He trusted that his intentions, rooted in love and justice, would ripple through the quantum field and inspire change. His faith wasn't passive; it was a force that moved millions to believe in a better future.

---

## Faith Beyond Logic

Faith transcends the boundaries of logic, often emerging as a bridge where reason falls short. While logic demands tangible evidence, faith draws its strength from trust and intuition. Many of life's most transformative experiences arise when we venture beyond what is known and embrace the uncertainties of the unknown. These are the moments when the quantum field resonates most powerfully, responding to the courage it takes to believe in possibilities that defy immediate proof. Faith invites the universe to collaborate in ways that logic alone cannot anticipate.

Consider an entrepreneur who invests in a bold idea despite the risks. Or a parent who trusts in their child's potential, even when the world sees only flaws. These acts of faith send powerful waves into the quantum field, shaping outcomes that logic alone could never achieve.

## Faith and the Subconscious Mind

Faith is more than a conscious decision; it's an energetic state that influences the subconscious mind. When you hold faith in your ability to achieve a goal, your subconscious begins to align your thoughts, emotions, and actions with that belief. This alignment strengthens your connection to the quantum field, amplifying your ability to manifest outcomes that match your intention. Faith, in this way, is a form of mental programming that rewires your inner world to reflect the reality you desire.

## When Faith Meets Resistance

Resistance often accompanies faith, testing your resolve and challenging your trust in the process. These moments are not signs to abandon your path but opportunities to deepen your faith. Resistance forces you to confront doubts, fears, and limiting beliefs that stand in the way of alignment. By meeting resistance with faith, you transform obstacles into stepping stones, strengthening your connection to the field.

## Faith in Everyday Life

Faith is not reserved for extraordinary circumstances; it is woven into the fabric of daily life. When you trust that your work will bear fruit, that your relationships will deepen, or that your health will improve, you are practicing faith. It's in the choices you make, the risks you take, and the dreams you nurture. Faith is the unseen hand that steadies you as you step into the unknown.

## Faith as Action

Faith isn't static; it's an active practice. It shows up in the way you speak, think, and act. Faith is deciding to take the leap, even when the net isn't visible. It's making choices that align with your intentions and trusting that the energy you put out will come back in ways that serve your highest good.

---

### Guided Reflection: Strengthening Faith

Think of an area in your life where you've struggled to trust the process. Close your eyes and visualize the outcome you desire, not as a distant possibility but as a certainty. Feel the emotions that come with achieving it—joy, gratitude, peace. Now, repeat to yourself: I trust in the process, and I am aligned with the field of infinite potential. Let this affirmation anchor your faith, carrying it into your thoughts and actions.

---

## Faith as a Collaborative Force

Faith operates as a dynamic partnership with the universe. When you set a clear intention and trust in its fulfillment, the quantum field responds, often orchestrating outcomes beyond your immediate foresight. Faith is not about exerting control over the process—it's about holding space for the universe to align with your energy and contribute its infinite creativity. This collaboration transforms faith into a dance of mutual resonance, where trust meets boundless potential.

## The Spiritual Depth of Faith

Faith is deeply spiritual, a connection to something greater than yourself. It's the trust that the Creator has a plan, that the universe is conspiring for your good. Faith aligns you with divine energy, allowing you to co-create in harmony with the greater whole. It's a reminder that you are never alone in your journey—that the field, the Creator, and the collective energy of existence are all working with you.

## Faith as a Legacy

The ripple effect of faith extends far beyond the individual. When you live with faith, you inspire others to believe in possibilities they may not have seen before. Think of figures like Gandhi, who moved millions with his unwavering belief in nonviolence, or Rosa Parks, whose faith in justice sparked a movement. These individuals remind us that faith isn't just personal—it's transformative, shaping realities for generations to come.

Faith, then, is not merely a feeling or a thought—it's a force. It's the current that carries you through uncertainty, the foundation that supports your dreams, and the key that unlocks the limitless potential of the quantum field. When you live with faith, you align your energy with creation itself, opening the door to a reality that is both intentional and divine.

# Revisiting the Core Concepts and Insights

**Belief** is not just a thought—it is the invisible architect of your reality. When you align belief with intention, you create a resonance that extends into the quantum field, shaping outcomes in ways that often defy logic. The placebo effect serves as a tangible example of this process, revealing that what the mind expects, the body and the universe often fulfill. The chemistry of belief—whether healing a body or manifesting a dream—is a testament to the profound connection between thought and creation.

**Faith,** too, plays a pivotal role. It's the quiet force that sustains intention when evidence of success is yet unseen. Faith is the bridge that carries you over the chasm of doubt, allowing you to step forward even when the path isn't fully illuminated. In its presence, resistance dissolves, and alignment strengthens, inviting the universe to work in concert with your desires. Faith transforms intention into action, action into resonance, and resonance into reality.

**Misaligned beliefs** act as static, distorting the signal you send into the quantum field. Reframing these limiting beliefs into empowering narratives not only clears the interference but also amplifies the clarity of your energy. When beliefs and faith merge with intention, they unlock doors you didn't even know existed, and the universe responds in kind, opening paths that align with your highest potential.

Throughout this journey, the recurring theme is **trust**—trust in your mind's ability to heal, trust in your intentions to manifest and trust in the quantum field to align with your energy. This trust is not blind; it's built on the understanding that belief isn't confined to the mind. It ripples outward, influencing not just your reality but the interconnected web of existence itself.

The intricate dance between belief, faith, and the quantum field reveals a profound truth: the universe doesn't simply react to your energy; it collaborates with it. The potential for transformation lies not in extraordinary efforts but in aligning with the subtle, unseen forces that shape reality. Trusting in this process, you begin to see that life isn't something that happens to you—it's something you co-create, one thought, one belief, one act of faith at a time.

And yet, the quantum field holds even deeper mysteries. Its principles—so often veiled in complex equations and abstract theories—carry profound spiritual implications. As we turn our gaze toward the experiments that have defined quantum physics, we begin to uncover a bridge between the theoretical and the divine, revealing a universe that is as much a canvas for spirituality as it is for science.

…

The connection between belief and reality is a testament to the universe's intricacy, but the story doesn't end there. Beneath the surface of our thoughts and intentions lies a web of quantum phenomena—experiments that challenge the boundaries of understanding and hint at truths far greater than themselves. From the paradoxes of observation to the mysteries of entanglement, these discoveries invite us to explore not just the mechanics of the quantum field but its profound spiritual significance.

Through their lens, we glimpse a universe that is as much a mirror of our consciousness as it is a playground of infinite potential.

# Chapter Nine

# Quantum Experiments and Their Spiritual Implications

*"If quantum mechanics hasn't profoundly shocked you, you haven't understood it yet. Everything we call real is made of things that cannot be regarded as real."*

– Niels Bohr

Imagine holding a box in your hands, knowing that within it lies both life and death, potential and reality, waiting for a single moment to be revealed. This is Schrödinger's cat—a paradox that reflects the infinite possibilities of our existence, shaped by observation and intention.

This isn't a riddle or a philosophical musing; it's one of the most famous thought experiments in quantum physics, and it challenges our very understanding of reality. Yet, it also points toward something extraordinary: the universe is not as fixed or as simple as it seems. Instead, it is filled with boundless potential, waiting for observation and intention to bring it to life.

This chapter takes us into the heart of quantum physics, exploring experiments that are as perplexing as they are profound. These scientific milestones not only expand our understanding of the quantum field but also reveal its spiritual implications. From the strange duality of *Schrödinger's cat* to the mind-bending effects of quantum erasure and entanglement, these phenomena demonstrate how deeply connected consciousness is to reality. They invite us to see the universe not as a static machine but as a living, breathing web of potential and interconnection.

# Schrödinger's Cat: Understanding Potentiality

## A Paradox in a Box

In 1935, Austrian physicist Erwin Schrödinger introduced a thought experiment that shook the foundations of science and philosophy. He described a sealed box containing a cat, a radioactive atom, a Geiger counter, and a vial of poison. If the atom decayed, the Geiger counter would release the poison, killing the cat. If the atom did not decay, the cat would remain alive. However, according to quantum mechanics, until the box is opened and the system observed, the cat exists in a superposition—both alive and dead at the same time.

This paradox illustrates a fundamental principle of quantum physics: *potentiality*. At its most basic level, the universe doesn't operate in absolutes but in probabilities. The act of observation determines which potential becomes reality.

> **Potentiality** is the concept that all possible states of a system exist simultaneously until observed or measured. This principle suggests that the act of observation collapses multiple possibilities into a single outcome. It underscores the dynamic and probabilistic nature of reality, where the universe operates as a field of probabilities rather than certainties.

## Observation as Creation

What does Schrödinger's cat have to do with your life? Everything. The thought experiment suggests that the universe is a sea of possibilities, and our focus—our observation—is what collapses potential into reality. When you focus your attention on a goal, you are metaphorically opening the box, choosing one outcome from a field of infinite possibilities. This isn't just theoretical; it's the essence of co-creation.

## The Power of Potential

The spiritual implications of potentiality are profound. They remind us that life is not predetermined, but fluid, responsive to our energy and intention. Every moment holds countless possibilities, like seeds waiting to be watered. Your focus is the sunlight that helps one seed grow while leaving others dormant. Schrödinger's cat challenges us to ask: What possibilities are we watering with our attention, and which are we leaving unopened in the box?

## A Practical Reflection

Think of a moment when you faced a decision. Perhaps you hesitated, unsure of what the outcome would be. That uncertainty was your own version of the cat in the box. Once you chose, the potential solidified into reality. The question is not just what you chose, but how you chose—did you act with faith and clarity, or fear and doubt? Your state of mind, like an observer in a quantum experiment, shapes the outcome more than you realize.

## Beyond the Paradox

Schrödinger's cat isn't meant to be solved; it's meant to be considered. It reminds us that we are both observers and participants in the universe's grand experiment. Whether through prayer, visualization, or meditation, the way we observe the quantum field determines the reality we experience. This isn't magic; it's the natural interplay of consciousness and creation.

## Stories of Observation and Potential

Real-life examples of this principle abound. Athletes preparing for a championship often speak of visualizing their performance down to the smallest detail—each movement, each victory. By mentally observing a desired outcome, they align their energy with that possibility, increasing its likelihood. The same principle applies to inventors, artists, and anyone with a dream. By focusing on potential, they bring it closer to reality.

Schrödinger's thought experiment, as abstract as it may seem, mirrors our everyday lives. Each moment is a box filled with potential. And with every choice, we play the role of observer, turning one possibility into reality while leaving others behind. The question isn't whether the cat is alive or dead—it's whether we are aware of the immense creative power we hold as observers in the quantum field.

When we approach life with this understanding, the quantum field begins to feel less like a mystery and more like an invitation—one that urges us to explore its depths with curiosity and intention. But the box of possibilities doesn't end here. Time, entanglement, and the very fabric of existence hold even greater wonders, as we shall soon discover.

# Delayed Choice and Quantum Eraser – Nonlinear Time and Observation

## The Universe's Split Decision

Imagine a beam of light passing through a double-slit experiment—a classic setup in quantum physics. When no one observes the light, it behaves like a wave, creating an interference pattern. But when scientists measure which slit the photon travels through, the light behaves like a particle, as if it "knows" it's being watched. This phenomenon alone is puzzling, but the delayed-choice experiment takes it one step further.

In this variation, the decision to measure or not measure the photon occurs after the photon has already passed through the slits. Astoundingly, the photon seems to retroactively *"choose"* its behavior based on the observer's later action. It's as though the photon's past depends on a future decision, challenging our very understanding of time.

## The Quantum Eraser

If the delayed-choice experiment wasn't enough to bend our perception of reality, the quantum eraser experiment adds another layer of intrigue. Here, the *"which-path"* information—the record of whether a photon went through one slit or the other—is erased after the photon has already hit the detection screen. When this information is erased, the interference pattern reappears, as if the photon "forgets" it was being observed.

> **Which-path** refers to determining the specific path a particle takes in experiments like the double-slit experiment. Observing the "which-path" information collapses the particle's wave-like behavior into particle-like behavior, illustrating the profound influence of observation on quantum systems.

These experiments suggest that time in the quantum world isn't linear. The past, present, and future seem to intertwine, influenced by observation and intention. The implications of this are staggering, not just scientifically but spiritually, as they hint that time may be less rigid and more fluid than we've been taught to believe.

> **Quantum Eraser** experiment demonstrates that information about a particle's "which-path" can be erased after it has been observed, causing particle-like behavior to revert back wave-like interference patterns. This suggests that the act of observation–and the availability of information–directly influences the behavior of quantum systems, even retroactively, challenging our conventional understanding of time and causality.

## Time as a Living Force

Time, as revealed by the quantum field, is not a rigid sequence but a fluid and responsive force, bending to the awareness and energy we bring to it. Like a river flowing in multiple directions, it carries with it the power to transform both the past and the future.

These experiments suggest that our actions in the present can ripple into the past and influence the future in ways we cannot yet fully grasp. This challenges the very core of cause and effect, hinting at a universe where time is not fixed but malleable, responding to the intentions and observations of conscious beings.

## Spiritual Implications

From a spiritual perspective, the nonlinear nature of time echoes ancient teachings about the eternal now. Many traditions emphasize that the present moment holds infinite power—not just to shape the future but to reconcile the past. The delayed-choice and quantum eraser experiments offer a scientific lens through which to view this truth. They suggest that the universe doesn't operate on a rigid timeline but responds dynamically to the energy and focus we bring into the moment.

## The Observer's Role in Time

If observation influences the past, it raises a profound question: how does our awareness shape not just what is to come, but what has already been? This idea resonates with practices like forgiveness and healing, where releasing negative emotions tied to past events seems to create a ripple of peace that transcends time. It also aligns with the notion that memories, often viewed as static, can transform through the lens of perspective and intention.

## A Real-World Parallel

Think of those moments when something you learn or experience seems to reframe a past event entirely. A conversation with a loved one or a new piece of information can shift your understanding of a memory, making it feel as though the past itself has changed. While this may not involve quantum physics, it reflects the malleability of perception and its ability to influence how we experience time.

---

## Reflective Exercise: Rewriting Your Past

Take a moment to reflect on a challenging memory. What would happen if you revisited it with a lens of compassion or gratitude? How might this shift the way you carry that experience into the present? Write down a new narrative for that memory, one that aligns with healing and growth. Consider how this act of reframing might influence your current reality.

---

### Co-Creating Through Time

The delayed-choice and quantum eraser experiments reveal a universe that isn't bound by the constraints of linear time. They suggest that the energy we project today doesn't just shape tomorrow—it reverberates into the past, creating a feedback loop of potentiality. This interplay between observation, intention, and time opens the door to a deeper understanding of our role as co-creators, not just of the present, but of the continuum in which we exist.

The quantum field responds to our awareness, weaving time into a fabric of infinite possibility. Whether through science or spirituality, the message is clear: the present moment is more powerful than we've ever imagined. It is the point of convergence where past and future meet, a gateway through which we can influence the flow of creation itself. And as we step deeper into this understanding, we find that the threads of time are not just connecting us—they are inviting us to participate in the unfolding story of the universe.

## The EPR Paradox – Exploring Quantum Entanglement

### An Unbreakable Connection

In 1935, Albert Einstein, along with Boris Podolsky and Nathan Rosen, posed a question that would shake the foundations of quantum mechanics. The EPR Paradox, as it came to be known, described a phenomenon so strange that Einstein himself called it "spooky action at a distance." They theorized that two particles, once entangled, could instantaneously influence one another, no matter how far apart they were. If one particle's state was measured, the state of its entangled partner would be determined instantly, even if separated by light-years.

What was most unsettling wasn't just the apparent violation of the speed of light. It was the implication that space and time, as we understand them, might not exist in the way we think. Instead, quantum entanglement suggested a deeper, invisible connection underlying the entire universe.

### The Science of Entanglement

Entanglement is more than a thought experiment—it has been demonstrated in numerous real-world studies. In 2022, for instance, researchers working with quantum computers successfully measured entangled photons, proving once again that changes to one particle instantly affected its twin. These results defy classical physics and hint at a hidden unity, a "quantum glue" that binds all things together.

This phenomenon isn't just theoretical. Entanglement is now being explored for revolutionary technologies like quantum computing and unhackable communication systems. But beyond its practical applications, it reveals something profound: the universe is fundamentally interconnected in ways we are only beginning to comprehend.

## The Spiritual Mirror

The concept of entanglement is more than a scientific curiosity—it mirrors spiritual truths taught for centuries. Many religious and philosophical traditions speak of oneness, the idea that all beings and all things are part of a single, unified whole. Quantum entanglement gives this ancient wisdom a modern, scientific context, showing that separation is, at best, an illusion. What happens to one affects the whole, not in metaphor, but in measurable reality.

Entanglement unveils a profound truth: that every thought, every action, and every soul is part of an intricate web of connection. It challenges us to see relationships not as separate threads but as vital strands in a shared fabric of existence.

If particles can remain connected across unimaginable distances, what does this say about the bond between our thoughts, actions, and the larger web of existence?

## Entanglement in Human Experience

Have you ever thought of someone, only to have them call you moments later? Or experienced a deep sense of connection with a loved one, even when they're far away? While these experiences are often dismissed as coincidence, they resonate with the principles of entanglement. The energy we share with others doesn't dissipate—it remains as a thread linking us through time and space.

A poignant example of this can be seen in studies of twins separated at birth. Despite living completely separate lives, many report eerily similar preferences, habits, and even life events. While this phenomenon is often attributed to genetics, it also suggests an unseen connection, one that science is still striving to understand.

---

### Reflective Exercise: Recognizing Your Connections

Take a moment to think of someone who holds a special place in your life. Reflect on a time when you felt deeply connected to them, even if you were apart. Write down how that connection has influenced your thoughts, emotions, or actions. Consider how this bond might extend beyond what is visible or measurable, forming part of the invisible fabric of your shared reality.

---

## Entanglement and the Quantum Field

On a quantum level, entanglement illustrates the interconnected nature of existence. But its implications extend far beyond physics. If all things are connected, then every action, thought, and intention sends ripples through the quantum field, touching lives and realities far beyond our immediate awareness. This isn't just a scientific idea—it's an invitation to live with greater mindfulness and compassion, knowing that everything we do contributes to the greater whole.

## A Cosmic Perspective

Entanglement shifts our perspective from individuality to unity. It reminds us that no one stands alone; we are all threads in the same universal tapestry. Whether through a kind word, a prayer, or a focused intention, our energy reaches farther than we can see, influencing not just the immediate present but the farthest edges of existence.

As we explore the spiritual implications of entanglement, we find that it's not just a phenomenon of particles but of people, communities, and the divine. The quantum field is a web, connecting every atom, every thought, every soul. And when we act in harmony with this truth, we step into our role as co-creators, not just of individual lives but of a shared reality that reflects the unity of all things.

The interconnectedness revealed through entanglement isn't confined to the quantum realm. It is woven into the very fabric of existence, bridging science, spirituality, and the profound mystery of being. It urges us to consider how deeply we are connected—not just to each other but to the infinite possibilities that exist within the quantum field. And in those connections, the story of creation continues to unfold.

# Orch-OR Theory – Consciousness as a Quantum Phenomenon

## The Mind as the Architect of Reality

For centuries, philosophers and mystics have pondered the nature of consciousness. What is it? Where does it come from? And how does it relate to the universe? Science, for much of its history, avoided these questions, preferring to focus on the tangible. But in the late 20th century, something extraordinary happened: consciousness found its way into quantum mechanics.

The *Orch-OR Theory,* short for *"Orchestrated Objective Reduction,"* suggests that consciousness arises not from the brain alone but from quantum processes occurring within it. The brain isn't just a machine made of neurons—it's a quantum instrument, capable of interacting with the fundamental fabric of reality.

## The Quantum Orchestra in Your Brain

The Orch-OR theory argues that microtubules, tiny structures within brain cells, act as quantum processors. Within these microtubules, quantum superpositions—states of potentiality—are said to collapse into a singular experience, creating what we perceive as consciousness. In essence, the brain orchestrates quantum events to produce thought, awareness, and perception.

What's revolutionary about this idea is its implication that consciousness isn't confined to the physical brain. Instead, it's a dynamic interaction between the quantum field and the structures of the brain—a bridge between the physical and the metaphysical.

## The Intersection of Science and Spirit

If consciousness is indeed rooted in quantum processes, it means our thoughts and intentions are more than electrical signals bouncing around in our skulls. They are energetic events, resonating with the quantum field and influencing the reality around us. This aligns with spiritual traditions that have long described the mind as a co-creator of existence, capable of shaping the universe through focus, intention, and belief.

The Orch-OR theory bridges science and spirituality, offering a framework where the material and the mystical are not separate but deeply intertwined. It suggests that the mind doesn't just observe reality—it participates in its creation.

## Consciousness Beyond the Brain

This theory also raises profound questions about life and death. If consciousness is rooted in quantum phenomena, it may not be limited to the brain's physical structures. Some researchers speculate that when the body dies, the quantum information in the microtubules could persist, connecting to the broader quantum field. Could this be a scientific explanation for near-death experiences or the soul's immortality?

While these ideas are speculative, they resonate with spiritual teachings about the eternal nature of the soul. The Orch-OR theory invites us to consider consciousness not as a byproduct of biology but as a fundamental aspect of the universe itself.

## The Creative Mind

Consider the moments when inspiration strikes—a sudden idea, a flash of insight, a feeling that something greater is at work. These experiences hint at the quantum nature of consciousness, where thoughts and creativity seem to emerge from an unseen source. They remind us that the mind is not merely a receiver but a transmitter, capable of accessing and influencing the quantum field.

This perspective aligns with the lives of great creators and visionaries. From Einstein's breakthroughs to Mozart's compositions, moments of genius often feel like a direct connection to something beyond oneself. Could these moments reflect the brain's ability to tap into the quantum field, harmonizing with the infinite potential of existence?

---

### Reflective Exercise: Connecting to the Field

Close your eyes and focus on a question or challenge in your life. Instead of searching for an answer, simply allow your mind to rest in stillness, open to inspiration. Picture your thoughts as ripples in the quantum field, reaching out and interacting with the universe's boundless intelligence. See what arises—not from effort but from quiet connection.

---

## A Universe of Consciousness

The Orch-OR theory paints a picture of a universe where consciousness is not an anomaly but a fundamental force, shaping and being shaped by the quantum field. It suggests that our thoughts are not isolated events but part of a greater symphony, resonating with the energy of existence itself.

This understanding transforms the way we view ourselves and our place in the cosmos. If consciousness is a quantum phenomenon, then every thought, intention, and belief is an act of creation. The mind becomes a sacred tool, capable of harmonizing with the divine and participating in the unfolding of reality.

The implications of this are as vast as the quantum field itself. Consciousness, no longer confined to the limits of biology, becomes a bridge between the seen and unseen, the material and the spiritual, the finite and the infinite. And as we step into this understanding, we find that the universe is not just a place we live in—it is a field of awareness, inviting us to co-create its ever-unfolding story.

## Revisiting the Core Concepts and Insights

Through the lens of quantum experiments, we are invited to step into a universe brimming with potential—a living, interconnected reality where our thoughts and intentions are the architects of creation. It is a call to awaken to the infinite possibilities within us and to embrace our role as co-creators of this divine masterpiece. **Schrödinger's cat** challenges us to confront the paradox of potentiality, where reality exists as a field of possibilities until observation collapses it into one outcome. This principle resonates with the idea that our focused intention shapes the world around us, urging us to take responsibility for the seeds of thought we cultivate.

The **delayed-choice** and **quantum eraser** experiments push this understanding even further, blurring the lines between past, present, and future. Time reveals itself not as a rigid sequence but as a dynamic, living entity. Every choice, every observation, ripples forward and backward, weaving the fabric of reality in ways that defy logic yet align beautifully with spiritual teachings about the eternal now. These revelations ask us to consider the weight of our choices—not just for what lies ahead, but for the echoes they send through the timeline of existence.

**Entanglement** offers a profound reminder of our interconnectedness, not just with one another but with the universe itself. This quantum bond defies the boundaries of space, affirming that separation is an illusion. What affects one particle affects the whole, just as the energy we project into the world reverberates through the cosmic web, influencing outcomes far beyond our immediate awareness. It's a call to live with mindfulness and compassion, understanding that our actions are threads in a shared tapestry.

The **Orch-OR theory** takes these insights to a deeply personal level, presenting consciousness as a quantum phenomenon that bridges the material and the metaphysical. The mind becomes a vessel for co-creation, interacting with the quantum field to shape reality itself. This connection suggests that our thoughts are not fleeting, insignificant sparks but powerful forces capable of harmonizing with the infinite potential of the universe.

Through these experiments and theories, we glimpse a universe that is far from mechanical or deterministic. It is a living, dynamic field of energy and awareness, where observation and intention create, time bends to consciousness, and connections transcend physical limitations. This understanding transforms not only how we view the cosmos but how we see ourselves within it—as active participants in an unfolding story of creation.

And yet, the mystery deepens. If the universe is so attuned to consciousness, what does it mean to live a life in harmony with this awareness? What does it look like to co-create not just in fleeting moments but as a lifelong practice, a sacred dialogue with the Creator? These questions beckon us forward, promising an even greater understanding of the divine processes at work in the quantum field and within our own hearts. The next step on this journey invites us to explore the profound responsibility and wonder of living as co-creators, in tune with the rhythms of existence and the whispers of the unknown.

And as we prepare to delve deeper, the questions linger: What does it mean to trust fully in the unseen forces at work? How do we navigate the dance of co-creation when the path is unclear? And how can we live in harmony with the sacred mystery of existence, allowing its wisdom to guide us toward a life of meaning, alignment, and divine connection?

These questions are not meant to be answered in haste. They are invitations to explore, to reflect, and to embrace the unfolding journey with an open heart. For the journey of co-creation is not a destination—it is a way of being, a continuous dialogue with the Creator, and a testament to the profound interconnectedness of all things.

As we step forward, the universe waits, ready to respond to the energy we bring to its infinite possibilities.

# Chapter Ten

# Co-Creation as a Lifelong Practice

*"Whatever we plant in our subconscious mind and nourish with repetition and emotion will one day become a reality."*
— Earl Nightingale

A poet once said, "We make the road by walking." And isn't that the truth? The art of co-creation is less a finished masterpiece and more a perpetual act of becoming—a dynamic conversation between ourselves and the divine. With every step and every choice, we etch our stories into the fabric of existence, leaving marks that ripple far beyond what we can see or understand.

Co-creation isn't a one-time event or a fleeting epiphany. It's a practice—a deliberate and ongoing partnership with the quantum field and the Creator. It asks for faith in forces unseen, for trust in the process even when the destination is unclear. This chapter delves into the lifelong commitment of co-creation, exploring how maintaining an open dialogue with the Creator, surrendering to the mysteries of existence, and marveling at the universe's intricate design can sustain a life lived in alignment with divine intention.

## Ongoing Conversation — Lifelong Connection to the Creator

The true beauty of co-creation lies in its constancy. It isn't confined to grand gestures or moments of heightened spirituality. It weaves itself into the fabric of our everyday lives, from the quiet prayer whispered before sleep to the fleeting thought of gratitude during a busy afternoon. Each of these moments is a thread in the ongoing tapestry of dialogue between the Creator and creation.

This conversation begins with intention. Every thought, every word, every action is a form of expression that the quantum field hears and responds to. Consider how artists shape clay into pottery or how musicians translate emotion into melody. They don't wait for the final product to appear; they engage in the act of creation, trusting the process to reveal something meaningful. The same is true for our partnership with the divine. We shape our lives not in one sweeping motion but in countless small, deliberate acts of intention and trust.

But a conversation, by definition, is two-sided. As we pour our energy into the quantum field, it responds—not always in the ways we expect, but often in ways that guide us toward growth and alignment. Sometimes, it speaks through synchronicities: the unexpected opportunity, the chance meeting, or the sudden insight that answers a question we didn't even know we were asking. Other times, it speaks through silence, inviting us to reflect, recalibrate, and rediscover the quiet power of faith.

## Rituals for Connection

How do we keep this dialogue alive? By nurturing it with intentionality. Daily practices like prayer, meditation, journaling, or even a walk in nature create the space for this exchange to flourish. They act as invitations for the Creator to enter our lives, to share wisdom and direction through the subtle language of intuition and inspiration.

Take the story of a man who felt lost in his career. Unsure of his next steps, he began writing down his thoughts and feelings each morning, addressing them to the universe as if writing a letter to an old friend. Over time, patterns emerged in his writing—dreams he had long forgotten, skills he wanted to develop. What began as a simple ritual became a compass, guiding him toward a career that aligned with his deeper purpose. His ongoing conversation with the divine didn't solve every problem overnight, but it opened doors he hadn't realized were there.

---

## Reflective Exercise: Strengthening the Dialogue

Find a moment of stillness and ask yourself: What is one area of my life where I feel disconnected? Close your eyes, take a deep breath, and mentally address this question to the Creator. Speak as if sharing with a trusted friend, allowing your words to flow freely. Then, release the question into the quantum field, trusting that the response will come—not necessarily in words, but in the opportunities, inspirations, or insights that follow.

---

The practice of ongoing conversation reminds us that co-creation is not a solitary endeavor. It is a partnership, a dance between the finite and the infinite, the known and the unknown. By engaging with it daily, we keep the channels open for divine wisdom to guide our path, enriching not just our lives but the lives of those around us.

# Faith in the Unseen – Trusting Divine Processes

## The Unseen Hand

Trust. It's an act of courage, especially when the outcome is uncertain. Faith in the unseen is not a blind leap but a steady walk forward, guided by an inner knowing that the universe is far more intricate than what meets the eye. The farmer planting seeds trusts the soil to nourish them, though he cannot see what happens beneath the surface. Similarly, faith asks us to plant intentions in the quantum field and believe that divine processes are at work, even when results are not immediately visible.

This faith is not passive; it is active engagement with life. It requires us to take steps forward, even when the full path remains hidden. Consider the traveler in the darkness, holding only a lantern. The light may illuminate just a few steps ahead, but those steps are enough to move forward. In the same way, faith guides us when logic falters, when doubts creep in, and when the way seems obscured by uncertainty.

## The Power of Letting Go

To trust the unseen, we must relinquish the illusion of control. It's tempting to map out every detail, to strive for certainty in a world that offers none. Yet the most profound moments of creation often arise not from control but from surrender. When we release our grip on outcomes and allow the quantum field to respond in its own time and way, we make space for possibilities we couldn't have imagined.

## | *A Story of Letting Go* |

Take **Steve Jobs**, co-founder of Apple, faced one of the most public and challenging rejections of his career when he was ousted from the very company he had helped create. For many, such a setback would signal defeat. But Jobs, instead of clinging to resentment or striving to control the narrative, embraced what he called "beginner's mind." He shifted his focus to exploring new creative ventures.

Jobs founded NeXT and purchased Pixar, where his passion for innovation and storytelling flourished. For a time, the success of Pixar overshadowed his contributions to technology. By letting go of his attachment to Apple and trusting the unfolding of his path, he grew in ways that wouldn't have been possible had he stayed in control of his original vision.

Years later, Apple brought him back, and his renewed leadership sparked the most innovative period in the company's history, introducing groundbreaking products like the iPhone and iPad. Jobs often reflected on how being fired was one of the best things that ever happened to him because it freed him to reimagine his role as a creator.

This illustrates how surrendering control can lead to outcomes far beyond what we initially envision.

---

## The Whisper of Divine Timing

Faith in the unseen also means trusting in timing. The universe doesn't operate on human schedules; it follows its own rhythms, often aligning events and opportunities in ways that are only clear in hindsight. How often do we find ourselves frustrated by delays, only to realize later that those delays were necessary for something greater to unfold?

Think about the teacher who applied for a leadership position at her school but was passed over in favor of another candidate. Disheartened, she questioned her worth. A year later, a position opened at a school with a mission that resonated deeply with her values. It was a better fit than she could have imagined, but it required patience and faith to arrive at that moment. The apparent setback had been a setup for something far greater.

## Faith Beyond Outcomes

True faith is not contingent on results. It does not say, "I will trust if I see proof."

It says, "I will trust because I believe in a higher order, a greater purpose." This kind of faith transcends circumstances. It allows us to remain grounded even when life's storms rage, confident that the unseen forces at work are aligning our lives with the divine.

This faith is mirrored in countless spiritual traditions. The psalmist writes of walking through the valley of the shadow of death, fearing no evil because of a divine presence. In quantum terms, this is the belief that even in the face of uncertainty, the field is responding to our energy, shaping outcomes that serve our growth and purpose.

## Reflective Exercise: Strengthening Trust

Think of a situation in your life where the outcome is unclear. Instead of focusing on what you can control, shift your attention to what you can release. Take a moment to close your eyes, breathe deeply, and visualize handing over your concerns to the Creator. Picture them as light, dissolving into the quantum field, where they are met with infinite possibilities. Feel the weight lifting as you trust that the unseen is working in your favor.

## The Freedom of Faith

Faith in the unseen frees us from the anxiety of needing to know everything. It allows us to live with open hearts, embrace the mystery of existence, and act with courage even when the outcome is uncertain. It transforms doubt into possibility, fear into hope, and hesitation into action.

This trust is not a one-time decision but a practice—a daily choice to believe in the unseen forces that guide us. It is the foundation of co-creation, the steady rhythm that keeps us aligned with the Creator's design. With faith, we step into the unknown not with fear but with wonder, knowing that we are held by something greater than ourselves. And as we take those steps, the path unfolds, revealing a life shaped by divine hands and infinite possibilities.

# Sacred Mystery – Embracing the Unknown

## The Invitation of the Unknown

There's a certain beauty in not knowing. Life, after all, is not a puzzle to be solved but a mystery to be lived. Sacred mystery invites us to release the need for certainty, to accept that some questions are meant to linger, and to find peace in the unanswered. It's the space between the notes in a symphony, the quiet pause before the dawn. The unknown isn't an obstacle to understanding—it's the fertile ground where wonder takes root.

Throughout history, humanity has grappled with the unknown, seeking answers in the stars, in sacred texts, and in the fabric of existence itself. And yet, for every answer we uncover, new questions arise. The quantum field is no exception. Its potentiality, its paradoxes, and its boundless possibilities remind us that some truths transcend the limits of logic. To embrace sacred mystery is to acknowledge that the universe is both knowable and unknowable, a dance of light and shadow that reflects the divine.

## Mystery as a Guide

Rather than fearing the unknown, what if we viewed it as a guide? The unknown doesn't demand our control; it asks for our trust. It beckons us to step forward, not because we see the full path but because we sense the presence of something greater leading us. Consider the explorers who sailed into uncharted waters, guided only by the stars and their faith in what lay beyond the horizon. Their journeys weren't defined by certainty but by the courage to embrace mystery.

In our own lives, we face uncharted waters every day. A career change, a new relationship, a difficult decision—each is a step into the unknown. Yet within that uncertainty lies possibility. Sacred mystery asks us to trust the process, to let go of the need for immediate answers, and to allow the journey to unfold in its own time.

## The Power of Wonder

Wonder is the natural response to mystery. It's the wide-eyed awe of a child seeing the ocean for the first time, the quiet reverence of gazing at the stars, the thrill of discovering something that defies explanation. Wonder keeps us humble. It reminds us that no matter how much we learn, there is always more to discover. And it connects us to the divine, for wonder is the language of the soul.

Albert Einstein said, *"The most beautiful experience we can have is the mysterious. It is the fundamental emotion that stands at the cradle of true art and true science."* His words capture the essence of sacred mystery: a call to marvel at the universe not just for its answers but for its infinite questions.

## Surrendering to Mystery

Embracing sacred mystery requires surrender—a willingness to release the illusion of control and accept that some things may never be fully understood. This surrender is not a sign of weakness but of strength. It is the recognition that our finite minds are part of an infinite design and that the Creator's wisdom extends far beyond our grasp.

Take the story of a woman who struggled with infertility for years. Despite countless treatments and setbacks, she found herself drawn to adoption, a path she had never considered. Though she didn't understand why her journey unfolded the way it did, she embraced it with faith. Years later, as she held her adopted child, she realized that the unknown had led her to a love deeper than she could have imagined. Her surrender to mystery didn't erase her pain, but it revealed a purpose that made the journey worthwhile.

---

## Reflective Exercise: Embracing the Unknown

Think of an area of your life where you feel uncertain or lost. Instead of seeking immediate answers, take a moment to sit with the question itself. Close your eyes and place your hands over your heart. Breathe deeply and silently acknowledge the unknown. Whisper to yourself, "I don't have to know everything. I trust in the unfolding." Allow yourself to rest in the peace that comes from surrendering to mystery.

---

## The Gift of Mystery

Sacred mystery is a gift—a reminder that the universe is vast, that life is complex, and that we are part of something far greater than ourselves. It asks us to approach the world with curiosity and humility, to seek understanding while honoring the questions that remain. It teaches us that not knowing is not a failure but an invitation to grow, to explore, and to trust.

By embracing sacred mystery, we open ourselves to wonder, to discovery, and to the divine. We learn to live with open hearts, accepting that some of life's greatest truths are meant to be experienced rather than explained. And as we surrender to the unknown, we find that it holds more than uncertainty—it holds grace, possibility, and the whisper of the Creator's presence.

# The Anthropic Principle – The Universe's Fine-Tuning for Life

## The Universe on a Razor's Edge

The stars hang in delicate balance, the planets spin in their orbits, and the conditions on Earth allow life to thrive. At first glance, it might seem like chance. But as we look closer, the universe reveals a striking truth: it is fine-tuned for life. This is the heart of the *Anthropic Principle*—the idea that the universe's fundamental constants and laws appear perfectly calibrated to allow for our existence.

Consider this: if the force of gravity were even slightly weaker, stars couldn't form. If it were stronger, they'd burn out too quickly for planets and life to develop. The charge of the electron, the expansion rate of the universe, the exact tilt of Earth's axis—all these factors align so precisely that they create a world not just capable of sustaining life but of inspiring wonder. Coincidence? Or something more?

## A Cosmic Signature

The fine-tuning of the universe feels like a signature, a mark of intention left by a Creator who wanted life to exist. Physicists marvel at the improbability of it all. How is it that the constants governing our reality—gravity, electromagnetism, nuclear forces—are set within such narrow ranges that even the slightest deviation would make life impossible? The odds are so staggering that many describe it as though the universe "knew" we were coming.

For people of faith, the Anthropic Principle resonates deeply. It suggests purpose, design, and an invitation to reflect on our role within this grand cosmic arrangement. The Creator didn't simply set the universe in motion; it seems, instead, that every detail was crafted with care as if the quantum field itself sang a song that led to the birth of stars, the blossoming of life, and the rise of human consciousness.

> **Anthropic Principle** suggests that the universe's physical constants and laws are finely tuned to allow for the existence of life, particularly human life. It posits that the universe must be compatible with the conscious beings observing it, because the universe's properties are intrinsically linked to conscious observation.

## Life's Fragile Symphony

Life, as we know it, exists on a razor's edge. The interplay of forces that sustain it is as fragile as a symphony performed in perfect harmony. Imagine an orchestra where every musician plays their part flawlessly, each note aligning with the next to create a masterpiece. But what happens if one instrument falls out of tune? The harmony collapses. So it is with the universe. Its constants and laws, like the instruments of an orchestra, must remain in perfect alignment for life to endure.

This symphony is not limited to physical forces. It extends to the intricate ecosystems of Earth, to the interconnected web of life, and to the profound interdependence of all living things. From the migration of birds to the blooming of flowers, from the currents of the oceans to the patterns of the weather, the universe pulses with a rhythm that sustains and celebrates life.

## A Glimpse of the Creator's Mind

The Anthropic Principle offers us a glimpse into the Creator's mind—not as a distant, abstract force but as an artist, an architect, a lover of life. This fine-tuning suggests a universe that isn't random but intentional, designed to nurture not just existence but consciousness, curiosity, and connection.

Take the story of Fred Hoyle, the astrophysicist who discovered that carbon—an essential element of life—could only form in stars under extremely specific conditions. Though Hoyle identified as an atheist, this discovery left him astonished. He famously remarked, *"A superintellect has monkeyed with physics, as well as with chemistry and biology."* His words reflect the awe inspired by the universe's design, even in those who approach it from a purely scientific perspective.

## Our Role in the Grand Design

If the universe is fine-tuned for life, then we, as co-creators, have a responsibility to honor and nurture that gift. This fine-tuning is not an accident; it is an invitation. It calls us to live in harmony with the natural world, to seek balance in our relationships, and to align our intentions with the greater purpose of existence.

Reflect on this: the same forces that govern the movement of galaxies also govern the beating of your heart. The same quantum field that sustains the stars sustains your thoughts, your dreams, and your actions. You are not separate from the universe's design; you are an integral part of it, a living expression of its harmony.

---

## Reflective Exercise: Feeling the Fine-Tuning

Step outside on a clear night and look up at the stars. Take a deep breath and let the vastness of the universe sink in. Consider how each light in the sky represents a system governed by precise forces, how those forces allow for life on Earth, and how you are part of that same system. Whisper a word of gratitude—not for answers, but for the awe of being part of this fine-tuned cosmos.

---

## The Dance of Faith and Science

The Anthropic Principle bridges the worlds of science and spirituality, inviting us to see the divine in the details of creation. It reminds us that faith and reason are not opposites but partners in a dance that explores the mysteries of existence. Through this lens, the universe becomes not just a collection of particles and forces but a sacred expression of divine intention.

By contemplating the fine-tuning of the universe, we step closer to the Creator—not as an abstract idea but as an active presence woven into the fabric of reality. And in that closeness, we find not just understanding but inspiration, a call to live in alignment with the harmony that sustains us all.

# Revisiting the Core Concepts and Insights

The rhythm of co-creation hums quietly beneath the surface of every moment, every choice, and every interaction. It is not a crescendo, a one-time climax, or a singular achievement—it is the melody of a life lived in partnership with the divine. Each of us is invited to step into this song, not as passive listeners but as active participants, shaping the notes and harmonies that define our days.

The **ongoing conversation** with the Creator asks for our presence, not perfection. It thrives on the simple acts of gratitude, the whispered prayers, the intentional steps toward alignment. As we build this connection, the quantum field responds, weaving threads of possibility into a tapestry of purpose. Trust in divine processes becomes the compass that guides us through uncertainty, reminding us that outcomes are not always ours to dictate but to receive with grace.

**Sacred mystery** is both a veil and a gift. It humbles us, expands our perspective, and invites us to embrace what cannot yet be understood. This isn't an abandonment of seeking but a celebration of the journey itself. The fine-tuning of the universe revealed through the **Anthropic Principle**, becomes a reminder that our lives are neither accidental nor isolated. Every detail, every interaction, every moment of being reflects a cosmic design too intricate to ignore.

The universe's harmony calls to our souls, asking us to tune our lives to its frequency. It whispers through the patterns of nature, the vastness of the stars, and the quiet moments of stillness where inspiration blooms. It calls us not to understand everything but to trust deeply, to act boldly, and to live as co-creators in a masterpiece that spans both the seen and unseen.

We find ourselves standing at the threshold of deeper exploration. Just as the universe is fine-tuned for life, so too are we equipped with tools to align our energy with the quantum field. The practice of co-creation is not abstract; it is tangible, rooted in actions and habits that bring us closer to resonance with the divine. From reflective journaling to the art of gratitude, from creative visualization to the movement of energy through intention, these tools illuminate the path forward.

...

The call now is to take these truths and bring them into practice, to let them shape not only our thoughts but our actions. Co-creation isn't confined to theory—it lives in the choices we make, the energy we project, and the alignment we pursue. What follows is a guide to the practical, an invitation to engage with life's infinite possibilities and to step boldly into the creative partnership that awaits.

# Chapter Eleven

# Practical Tools for Co-Creation

*"Gratitude is not only the greatest of virtues
but the parent of all others."*

– Cicero

Think of your life as a blank canvas, each day a fresh opportunity to add color, depth, and meaning to the masterpiece. The quantum field is the palette, rich with possibilities, and the brush lies in your hands. But to create with intention, you need the right tools—simple yet profound practices that align your energy with the limitless potential of the universe.

The art of co-creation isn't confined to the abstract. It thrives in the tangible, in the daily rhythms and small rituals that connect us to the divine. By reflecting through journaling, cultivating gratitude, activating creative imagination, and aligning energy through movement and intention, we engage the quantum field with purpose. These tools are not only practical but transformational, empowering you to participate in the grand symphony of creation.

## Journaling – Reflecting and Aligning with Divine Energy

### A Dialogue with the Divine

Journaling is more than pen on paper; it is a sacred dialogue, a conversation between your conscious mind and the vast wisdom of the quantum field. When we write, we give shape to our thoughts, transforming scattered ideas into focused intention. The act itself is grounding, pulling the infinite into the tangible, bridging the gap between what is and what could be.

## The Power of Reflection

Consider the mind as a cluttered room. Journaling serves as a way to organize, to clear away the noise, and to uncover what truly matters. When you write about your dreams, fears, and desires, you begin to understand the patterns of your thoughts and emotions. More importantly, you become aware of how those patterns influence your energy and align—or misalign—you with the field.

For instance, someone reflecting on a persistent challenge might uncover a limiting belief that has shaped their actions. By identifying it, they gain the power to reframe, to replace doubt with faith, and resistance with trust. Journaling turns the act of reflection into a key for unlocking the door to transformation.

## A Daily Practice

You don't need elaborate prompts or a perfect setting to begin. Start small: write about what you're grateful for, what you want to create, or the emotions that surfaced during your day. Be honest, even if what comes out feels messy. The process is the point, not the product.

Set aside a few minutes each morning or evening. Treat this time as sacred—a moment to pause, reflect, and connect with the energy around you. Over time, your journal will become a map of your journey, a testament to the ways in which your intentions have shaped your reality.

### | *Stories of Transformation Through Writing* |

Consider the story of a man who, feeling stuck in his career, began writing letters to his future self. Each letter described the life he envisioned, the opportunities he wanted, and the person he aspired to become. Weeks turned into months, and as he reread his words, he noticed a shift—not just in his circumstances but in his mindset. The act of writing clarified his intentions and aligned his actions with his dreams. Within a year, he found himself living the life he had once only written about.

Writing letters to one's future self has long been a practice embraced by individuals seeking personal growth and clarity. For instance, Rachel Syme, a writer and journalist, initiated *"Penpalooza"* during the pandemic, connecting thousands through letter writing. This initiative not only fostered community but also highlighted the introspective power of writing.

Similarly, the website FutureMe.org has enabled countless individuals to send letters to their future selves, capturing their current thoughts, goals, and dreams. Many users have reported profound realizations upon reading their letters years later, noting how the act of writing helped manifest their envisioned futures.

These examples underscore the transformative potential of writing to one's future self, serving as a bridge between present intentions and future realities.

## Reflective Exercise: Writing Your Intentions

Take a moment now to grab a notebook or a blank sheet of paper. Write at the top: "What do I want to create?" Let your thoughts flow freely, without judgment. Write as if speaking directly to the quantum field, describing not only what you desire but how it feels to already have it. When you finish, read your words aloud. Feel the energy of your intentions resonate as though they are already unfolding.

Journaling is a practice of alignment. It calls you to slow down, to listen deeply, and to co-create with purpose. In the pages of your journal, you meet the quantum field not as an abstract concept but as a living, breathing presence, ready to reflect your energy back to you. And so, as your pen moves across the page, the Creator whispers, "What will we create today?"

## Gratitude Practices — Amplifying Resonance

### The Frequency of Gratitude

Gratitude is more than a fleeting feeling; it's a frequency—a vibration that resonates powerfully with the quantum field. When you engage in genuine appreciation, you align your energy with abundance, creating a ripple effect that draws more to be grateful for into your life. Gratitude, in its essence, is a way of saying to the universe, "I see your goodness, and I am open to more."

## The Science of Appreciation

Modern research supports what ancient wisdom has long proclaimed: gratitude transforms. Neuroscientists have found that regularly practicing gratitude rewires the brain, shifting focus from scarcity to abundance. This neurological shift isn't just emotional; it's energetic. Gratitude creates coherence in the heart, a state measurable through tools like heart rate variability monitors. When your heart is in a state of coherence, it sends signals to the brain and the quantum field, amplifying the resonance of your intentions.

## Everyday Gratitude, Extraordinary Results

Gratitude doesn't require grand gestures. It's in the small moments—the warmth of sunlight on your skin, the laughter of a friend, the quiet peace of an evening sky. A grateful heart finds abundance in what is rather than waiting for something more. When you consistently anchor yourself in appreciation, you shift your perspective and your energy, transforming how you experience the world and how the world responds to you.

Consider a struggling entrepreneur who began each day listing three things he was grateful for. At first, the list felt forced, his mind weighed down by worries. But as the days turned into weeks, he noticed a change. His focus shifted from obstacles to opportunities, and he began to attract clients and collaborators who resonated with his renewed energy. Gratitude didn't solve his challenges overnight, but it created a fertile ground for solutions to grow.

## Gratitude as a Spiritual Practice

Gratitude is also a form of prayer. It is the recognition of blessings already received, a silent thank-you to the Creator for the infinite possibilities that await. When we focus on gratitude, we acknowledge the divine presence in the ordinary, transforming even mundane moments into sacred ones. This practice becomes a dialogue with the quantum field, affirming our trust in its abundance.

## Creating a Gratitude Practice

To amplify resonance through gratitude, start with a simple practice. Each morning or evening, write down three things you're grateful for. Be specific. Instead of writing, "I'm grateful for my family," write, "I'm grateful for the way my daughter's smile lights up the room." This specificity deepens the emotional connection and strengthens the energetic vibration.

As you write, pause to feel the gratitude in your heart. Let it grow, expanding beyond the words on the page. Carry this energy with you throughout the day, allowing it to shape your interactions and intentions. Over time, you'll notice that gratitude becomes a lens through which you see the world—a lens that magnifies abundance and diminishes lack.

## Reflective Exercise: Heart-Centered Gratitude

Close your eyes and place your hand over your heart. Think of one thing you are deeply grateful for. As you hold this thought, take slow, deep breaths, feeling your heart expand with each inhale. With each exhale, send your gratitude into the quantum field like a wave rippling outward. Hold this feeling for a few moments, then open your eyes, carrying this resonance into the rest of your day.

Gratitude is not just a response to the good in life; it is a catalyst for more good to come. It shifts your energy, aligns your intentions, and creates a resonance that the universe cannot ignore. The quantum field, like a mirror, reflects back what you project, and a heart filled with gratitude becomes a beacon for abundance. When you speak the language of gratitude, the universe listens, responding with echoes of blessings yet to unfold.

## Creative Imagination – Exploring Quantum Possibilities

### The Canvas of the Mind

Your imagination is not mere whimsy—it is the birthplace of reality. The mind's ability to visualize, to craft vivid scenarios, is not confined to daydreams. Instead, it serves as a conduit to the quantum field, a way to shape the energy of possibility into tangible outcomes. Every innovation, every leap of progress, every personal transformation begins as a seed planted in the soil of imagination.

### The Power of Mental Creation

When you use your imagination with intention, you step into the role of co-creator. The quantum field is responsive, a realm teeming with potential, waiting to align with the energy you project. Visualizing your desired reality is like sketching the blueprint of a dream home before the foundation is laid. The clearer the vision, the stronger the alignment between thought and outcome.

Athletes understand this principle well. Many practice mental rehearsal, visualizing their performance in vivid detail before ever stepping onto the field or court. Studies show that this mental preparation activates the same neural pathways as physical practice, enhancing performance. When the mind rehearses success, the body follows, bridging the gap between imagination and reality.

## | *Stories of Creative Visualization* |

Consider **Walt Disney**, a man who built an empire on imagination. Long before Disneyland opened its gates, Disney visualized every detail—the sights, the sounds, the joy it would bring to families. He famously walked visitors through an empty lot, describing attractions that existed only in his mind. His ability to hold this vision unwaveringly turned a barren field into *"the happiest place on Earth."* Disney's story is a testament to how imagination fuels action and aligns the quantum field to manifest dreams.

And then there is the journey of **Kim Vaccarella**, a New Jersey entrepreneur who, during a family beach holiday in 2008, envisioned a solution to the common problem of disorganized and flimsy beach bags. She imagined a durable, stylish tote that could withstand sand and water while carrying all the essentials for a family outing. Despite lacking formal product development experience, Kim's clear vision guided her through the creation of a prototype and the subsequent launch of *Bogg Bag*. Her unwavering belief in her product attracted collaborators and resonated with consumers, transforming her idea into a thriving business that has sold over 3 million bags and is projected to reach $100 million in revenue.

These stories illustrates how a clear and focused vision can serve as a powerful catalyst in bringing an idea to life, even in the face of challenges.

## Imagination as a Spiritual Act

Creative imagination is also an act of faith. To envision a reality that does not yet exist requires trust in the unseen and belief in the quantum field's responsiveness. It is a silent prayer, a way of asking the Creator, "What if?" and waiting expectantly for the answer. Through imagination, we align with divine creativity, participating in the sacred act of bringing form to formlessness.

## Engaging Your Creative Power

Start small. Close your eyes and picture a single, specific moment of the life you want to create. See it clearly—the colors, the textures, the sounds. Feel the emotions tied to this moment as if it were already real. Then, take one tangible step that aligns with this vision. The quantum field responds not just to thought but to action guided by thought, turning possibility into progress.

## Reflective Exercise: The Perfect Day

Take a moment to reflect on your ideal day. Where are you? What are you doing? Who are you with? Write or visualize the details, allowing yourself to feel the joy and fulfillment of this imagined experience. As you hold this vision, know that every thought is a brushstroke on the canvas of your reality.

Creative imagination is not confined to the realm of fantasy; it is a tool for transformation. It allows you to explore quantum possibilities, aligning your thoughts with the life you are meant to create. The quantum field doesn't differentiate between what is and what could be—it simply responds to the energy you project. When you dare to imagine, you invite the Creator to dream with you, co-authoring a reality rich with possibility.

# Energy Flow – Harnessing Movement and Intention

## The Dance of Energy

Energy, like water, thrives in movement. When it stagnates, it loses its vibrancy and potential, but when it flows, it nourishes and transforms. This principle applies not only to rivers and currents but to the energy within you. Aligning with the quantum field requires more than stillness of mind; it often calls for the deliberate movement of the body and intention. Through physical practices and conscious action, you harmonize the energy around you, unlocking pathways to alignment and creation.

## The Body as a Conduit

Your body is more than a vessel; it is a dynamic energy system. Ancient traditions such as *Tai Chi, Qi Gong*, and yoga have long recognized the interplay between movement and energy flow. These practices emphasize deliberate, mindful motion to clear blockages, balance energy, and enhance connection to the universe.

When the body moves in harmony, it becomes a bridge to the quantum field, amplifying the resonance of your intentions.

Consider a musician tuning an instrument before a performance. The act of fine-tuning is not separate from the music but essential to its creation. In the same way, aligning your body's energy through movement prepares you to engage with the symphony of the universe. Each stretch, each breath, becomes a note, harmonizing with the vibrations of the field.

## Action as Alignment

Movement is not confined to physical practices; it also encompasses the actions you take in daily life. The quantum field responds to intention, but intention without action is like planting seeds without watering them. To harness the flow of energy, you must align your actions with your vision. Whether it's a simple step forward in pursuit of a goal or an act of kindness toward another, every action carries energy into the field, reinforcing your connection to creation.

Consider the story of a marathon runner who trained not just with her body but with her mind and spirit. Each step during her runs was an affirmation of her strength, her determination, and her alignment with the goal she sought to achieve. On race day, she didn't just run; she flowed, her energy synchronized with her intention. She crossed the finish line, not just as a testament to her physical endurance but as a demonstration of energy in motion, aligned with purpose.

## Movement as Meditation

Movement, when approached with mindfulness, becomes a meditation. A walk in nature, for example, is not merely exercise but an opportunity to align with the rhythms of the earth. Each step becomes a conversation with the quantum field, each breath a renewal of your connection to the present moment. Through movement, you dissolve distractions, channeling your energy into the flow of creation.

---

## Reflective Exercise: Moving with Intention

Stand in a quiet space and close your eyes. Take a deep breath and feel your feet connect with the ground beneath you. Begin to move slowly—a stretch, a sway, a step—letting each motion flow naturally. With each movement, set an intention: "I release what no longer serves me," or "I embrace the energy of creation." Feel the energy within you begin to circulate, connecting you to something greater.

---

### | *Stories of Energy Flow* |

**Sophia Andelight**, originally from Italy and now residing in London, began her yoga journey in 2001 with Kundalini yoga. Facing a challenging period in her life, she turned to daily practice, which not only improved her physical health but also transformed her entire life perspective. Through consistent movement and meditation, Sophia found clarity in moments of doubt, strength during challenges, and a deeper connection to the divine. She often describes her yoga mat as a sacred space where intention meets energy, facilitating profound

---

Energy flow reminds us that creation is not a static process. It requires movement—of body, of thought, of spirit. Whether through deliberate practices or the everyday actions that align with your vision, harnessing energy flow deepens your connection to the quantum field. And as you move, the universe moves with you, responding to each intention with the infinite potential of creation.

## Revisiting the Core Concepts and Insights

The journey of co-creation is not an abstract endeavor; it is a practical and transformative dance between intention and reality. Each of the tools explored in this chapter reveals a unique aspect of this dynamic process, reminding us that creation is as much about alignment as it is about action. Together, they form a framework for living in harmony with the quantum field, empowering us to take part in the ongoing dialogue between the human spirit and divine potential.

Through **journaling,** the act of self-reflection becomes a sacred practice. It is not just about recording thoughts but about uncovering truths. Each word written is a step toward clarity, helping to distill fleeting moments of inspiration into actionable insights. By putting pen to paper, you create a dialogue with the Creator, offering your intentions while opening yourself to receive divine guidance. It is in these moments of stillness that the seeds of transformation take root, ready to flourish with care and attention.

**Gratitude**, too, reveals itself as more than a polite gesture. It is an energy that amplifies and attracts, an acknowledgment of abundance that opens the door to even greater blessings. When you align yourself with gratitude, you raise your vibration, resonating with the frequencies of love, peace, and possibility. Like tuning an instrument to its perfect pitch, gratitude aligns your energy with the harmonious rhythms of the quantum field, making it a cornerstone of the co-creative process.

**Creative imagination** invites us to dream boldly. It reminds us that the mind is not confined by what is but is free to explore what could be. This freedom is the essence of divine co-creation, where thought becomes form, and intention becomes reality. Whether you're envisioning a personal goal or a collective shift, your imagination serves as a powerful bridge, connecting the world you see to the world you aspire to create.

**Movement**, both physical and intentional, demonstrates that energy thrives in flow. Stagnation hinders connection, while deliberate action breathes life into your intentions. From the graceful practice of yoga to the purposeful steps you take toward your goals, every movement carries energy into the quantum field, reinforcing your commitment to creation. Movement is not just about doing; it's about being—in alignment, in harmony, and in tune with the divine forces that guide and support your journey.

As these tools weave together, they illuminate a truth that is both empowering and humbling: co-creation is not a one-time event but a lifelong practice. It is a rhythm, a dance, a continuous exchange of energy between you and the Creator. The quantum field responds to your thoughts, actions, and intentions, but it also asks something of you—faith. Faith that the unseen forces at work are guiding you. Faith that your alignment will lead to fulfillment. Faith that even when the path is unclear, the way forward will reveal itself in time.

Through this practice, you begin to understand that you are not merely an observer of life but an active participant in its unfolding. Your thoughts and actions ripple through the quantum field, touching lives you may never meet and influencing outcomes you may never see. This is the essence of co-creation: the recognition that your life is intricately connected to a greater whole and that your alignment has the power to shape not only your reality but the collective reality of the universe.

...

Life, as we've seen, is an ongoing dialogue with the divine, a series of moments that call us to align, to act, and to trust. Yet, there is another layer to this conversation—one that goes beyond personal creation and into the realm of service.

As you deepen your alignment with the quantum field, you may find yourself compelled to extend this energy outward, becoming a vessel for healing, harmony, and transformation. What if the next step is not about what you create for yourself but about what you offer to the world?

Let's explore this possibility.

# Chapter Twelve

# Serving as a Divine Vessel

*"Only a life lived for others is a life worthwhile."*
– Albert Einstein

There are moments when life presents a choice: to serve ourselves or to serve a greater good. These moments, subtle as whispers or as profound as thunder, often define who we are. To serve is not merely an act of charity; it is a sacred offering, a channeling of divine energy into a world longing for healing. When we become vessels for the Creator's intent, our actions ripple far beyond what the eye can see, touching lives, igniting change, and amplifying harmony in ways we may never fully understand.

This chapter explores what it means to serve as a divine vessel, not as an obligation but as a calling. Service is the highest expression of co-creation, aligning individual purpose with universal harmony. Through the intentional transmission of healing energy, the ripple effects of our actions, and the profound shifts brought by quantum resonance, we discover how to amplify the Creator's work through aligned intention and effort.

## Healing Energy: Transmitting Well-Being Through Intention

Healing begins where intention meets energy. It is a quiet force, unseen yet deeply felt, like the warmth of sunlight on a cold morning. To transmit healing energy is to channel the divine presence within, offering it freely to a world often burdened by pain and disconnection.

## The Power of Intention

In the quantum field, intention acts as a blueprint for creation. When directed with purpose and love, it becomes a conduit for healing, capable of touching lives at levels we may never witness. Research in energy healing, from Reiki to prayer studies, suggests that directed thought and emotion can influence physical and emotional well-being. This is not the stuff of superstition but a principle grounded in the interconnected nature of existence.

Consider the stories of nurses and caregivers who speak of holding a patient's hand, radiating calm and compassion. They often describe moments when the patient's pain seems to ease, their breathing slows, or peace washes over their face. These moments reveal the transformative power of intention—how the energy we project can guide others toward healing.

---

## Reflective Practice: Sending Healing Energy

Close your eyes and picture someone you know who is struggling, whether physically, emotionally, or spiritually. Take a deep breath, and as you exhale, visualize a soft, golden light emanating from your heart. This light carries your intention for their healing and well-being. Imagine it enveloping them, filling the spaces where pain or fear once lingered. This practice, simple yet profound, reminds us that healing energy is not bound by distance or circumstance.

---

## Healing Beyond the Physical

While physical healing is tangible, emotional and spiritual healing often occurs quietly, in the spaces between words and actions. When we offer a kind gesture, listen without judgment, or simply hold space for someone, we transmit healing energy that can mend fractures no medicine can touch. These moments of connection remind us that to heal another is to reaffirm our shared humanity.

## The Divine Nature of Healing

To serve as a healer is to act as a vessel for divine energy. This does not require credentials or mystical abilities but a willingness to be present and intentional. Whether through touch, words, or silent prayer, each act of healing aligns us with the Creator's work, making the world a little brighter, a little more whole.

Healing, in its truest form, is a gift both given and received. As we channel energy into others, we often find that our own spirits are lifted and our own burdens lightened. This reciprocity is the Creator's quiet way of reminding us that in serving others, we, too, are healed.

# Ripple Effect: Spreading Alignment to the Collective

Throw a single pebble into a still pond, and its ripples will extend far beyond where the pebble lands. The ripple effect, simple yet profound, mirrors how our actions—rooted in alignment—extend beyond ourselves, touching lives we may never know and shaping a world we may never see.

## The Interconnected Nature of Actions

Every act of service, no matter how small, sends waves of energy into the quantum field. Whether it's holding the door for a stranger, offering a comforting word, or dedicating time to a cause, these actions create a resonance that others unconsciously pick up. The field doesn't distinguish between big or small—it amplifies intention, allowing it to reach further than we might expect.

Consider the story of a young girl who, moved by the struggles of stray animals in her neighborhood, began crafting homemade shelters. Her simple act of kindness inspired neighbors to donate supplies, and soon, a community-wide initiative to care for homeless animals emerged. What began as one person's compassionate impulse evolved into a collective effort, transforming not only the animals' lives but the community's sense of connection and purpose.

## The Science of Ripples

Research into emotional contagion—the idea that feelings spread among groups like wildfire—underscores the power of the ripple effect. Studies reveal that one person's kindness or positivity can influence the mood of an entire room, which in turn influences the next interaction those people have, creating a cascading effect. What we project, the field magnifies.

In the quantum world, entanglement reminds us that particles, once connected, remain influenced by each other regardless of distance. Likewise, our actions, infused with intention, resonate through the invisible threads of connection that bind us all, subtly influencing outcomes we may never witness.

### Service as a Catalyst for Collective Healing

Aligned actions—those born from love, compassion, and service—do more than help individuals. They set a precedent, creating models of behavior that others instinctively follow. A single act of forgiveness, for instance, can ripple through a fractured family, mending relationships across generations. A community's decision to prioritize sustainability can inspire other cities to do the same, multiplying its impact.

These ripples do not stop at human borders. Nature itself responds to acts of alignment. From reforestation projects that revive dying ecosystems to the global shift toward renewable energy, our actions resonate with the planet, amplifying healing across species and landscapes.

---

## Reflective Exercise: Identifying Your Ripples

Take a moment to think about a time when someone else's action—large or small—changed your day or even your perspective. Now, consider a moment when you did the same for someone else, perhaps without realizing it. Reflect on how these ripples intersect, creating waves of energy that bind us in a shared experience. What ripple will you send next?

---

### The Divine Ripple Effect

Scriptures and spiritual traditions often speak of the mustard seed—a small, seemingly insignificant object that grows into something far greater. This metaphor reminds us that even the smallest aligned action, performed with love, holds infinite potential. It's a call to serve, not because we seek acknowledgment but because we trust that the energy we release will reach where it is needed most.

When we act in harmony with divine purpose, our ripples are not just personal—they are cosmic. They resonate with the quantum field, amplifying love, healing, and unity on a scale far beyond our comprehension.

## Service to the Whole: Actions Benefiting Universal Harmony

Service is the heartbeat of harmony, the bridge between intention and action. It is the expression of divine alignment in a tangible way, an offering of our energy to the collective good. When we shift our focus from "me" to "we," something profound occurs—not only within us but in the world we touch. The act of serving the whole transforms both the giver and the receiver, creating a cycle of resonance that echoes through the quantum field.

## The Call to Serve

Throughout history, individuals who answered the call to serve have left indelible marks on humanity. Think of Mahatma Gandhi, whose life of nonviolence inspired millions to seek justice through peace, or Mother Teresa, who saw divinity in the faces of the forgotten and devoted her life to their care. Their actions were not driven by ambition but by an unshakable belief in the power of service to heal, connect, and elevate.

But service is not reserved for saints. It is as accessible as offering your time to a neighbor, your skills to a cause, or your presence to someone in need. These acts, though they may seem small, contribute to the greater harmony of the whole. They are the threads that weave the fabric of unity, strengthening the bonds that hold us together.

## The Quantum Perspective

From a quantum lens, every action is a vibration sent into the field, interacting with countless others to create patterns of energy. When our actions align with the frequencies of compassion, generosity, and love, they harmonize with the vibrations of others, creating coherence. This coherence amplifies their impact, spreading far beyond what we might see or measure.

It is here that science and spirituality meet. Quantum entanglement tells us that particles, once connected, remain so no matter the distance. Likewise, our service connects us to others in ways that transcend time and space. A single act of kindness in one corner of the world may inspire hope in another, rippling through the interconnected web of existence.

## The Joy of Giving

Service is not a burden; it is a gift. Those who serve often speak of the joy they receive in return, a sense of fulfillment that no material possessions can match. This joy arises because service aligns us with our true nature as co-creators in a divine symphony. It reminds us that we are part of something greater than ourselves, a living, breathing whole that thrives when its parts work together in harmony.

Consider a teacher who dedicates their life to nurturing the minds of children.

The knowledge they impart, the encouragement they give, and the example they set shape not only the lives of their students but the future they will help create. Or think of the volunteer who spends their weekends planting trees in a barren field, knowing that they may never sit in their shade but understanding the legacy they leave for generations to come.

---

## Reflective Exercise: A Life of Service

Pause and reflect on the ways you currently serve others. Do you share your time, your talents, and your love? What more might you offer if you trusted that every act of service, no matter how small, contributes to the harmony of the whole? Let this reflection guide your next steps as you seek to align your actions with the needs of the collective.

---

### Serving the Divine

To serve the whole is to serve the divine. It is to recognize that every being, every element of creation, is an expression of the Creator's energy. When we serve, we participate in a sacred exchange, giving of ourselves to uplift others and, in turn, receiving the blessings of connection, purpose, and peace.

True service does not seek recognition or reward. It seeks only to give, trusting that the energy released will find its way back, multiplied. It is an act of faith, a testament to the power of love in motion. In serving the whole, we become vessels for divine energy, amplifying its reach and resonance.

## Quantum Resonance: Amplifying Global Shifts Through Aligned Actions

Every action we take sends ripples into the quantum field, but when those actions align with divine intention, the impact becomes transformative. This is quantum resonance—the phenomenon where frequencies in harmony amplify each other, creating waves of energy that extend far beyond their point of origin. As individuals tune their thoughts, actions, and intentions to higher frequencies, the collective field begins to resonate, amplifying change on a global scale.

### The Mechanics of Resonance

In physics, resonance occurs when one object vibrating at a certain frequency causes another to vibrate in sync. Think of a singer shattering glass with their voice.

The glass doesn't break because of the sound's volume but because the singer matches the glass's natural frequency, magnifying its vibration to the point of transformation. Similarly, in the quantum field, when we align our energy with divine love, compassion, and purpose, we become catalysts for shifts in the collective field.

This is not an abstract idea. Studies in group meditation, like those conducted by the HeartMath Institute, have shown measurable reductions in violence and stress when large numbers of people focus on peace and coherence. These outcomes suggest that our collective intentions, when resonating in harmony, can create tangible changes in the world around us.

## The Power of Collective Action

Now, picture a single drop falling into a still pond. Its ripples spread outward, touching every corner of the surface. Add more drops, each falling in alignment, and the ripples amplify, creating waves of motion. This is the essence of quantum resonance in collective action. When individuals come together with aligned intentions—whether in meditation, prayer, or unified purpose—their energy combines, amplifying their impact and creating waves of transformation.

Consider the story of global movements for change. Whether it's a march for civil rights, a prayer vigil for peace, or an environmental initiative, these efforts often begin with a small group of aligned individuals. Their resonance, fueled by shared purpose, spreads like wildfire, inspiring others and magnifying their influence until the entire world takes notice. What starts as a whisper becomes a roar, echoing through the quantum field.

## Your Role in the Resonance

Each of us plays a part in this symphony of resonance. Our individual actions, no matter how small, contribute to the collective vibration. A kind word, a selfless act, or a moment of prayer sends energy into the field, connecting with similar frequencies and amplifying their reach. When we align our actions with the divine, we become instruments of change, adding our unique notes to the universal melody.

Reflect for a moment: What frequencies are you sending into the quantum field? Are they aligned with love, gratitude, and compassion, or do they echo fear, doubt, or dissonance? The beauty of resonance is its ability to shift. By recalibrating your intentions and actions, you can amplify the energy you wish to see in the world.

### A Global Symphony

Quantum resonance reminds us that we are never isolated. Our thoughts and actions intertwine with those of others, creating a web of connection that spans the globe. This connection is both a responsibility and a gift. It challenges us to act with intention, knowing that our energy affects not only ourselves but the collective whole. It also offers the profound reassurance that we are part of something greater, a living network of divine energy working together to shape reality.

---

## Reflective Exercise: Tuning to the Collective Field

Close your eyes and take a moment to visualize the collective field as a vast ocean of energy. Picture your thoughts and actions as waves, contributing to its motion. What kind of ripples are you creating? Consider an action you can take today—whether small or large—that aligns with your highest intentions and adds to the resonance of love, harmony, and creation. Let this be your offering to the collective symphony.

---

Quantum resonance is both humbling and empowering. It reveals the interconnectedness of all things and invites us to step into our roles as co-creators of global harmony. When our actions resonate with divine purpose, their impact is magnified, touching lives in ways we may never see but can always trust.

## Revisiting the Core Concepts and Insights

Every step toward becoming a divine vessel is both a privilege and a calling. It is the recognition that our actions, words, and intentions ripple through the quantum field, shaping not just our personal reality but the shared experience of all. The journey begins with **healing energy**, a gift born from the profound understanding that our focused intention can channel well-being into the lives of others. Through prayer, meditation, or simple acts of kindness, we participate in an exchange of energy that transcends the physical, entering the unseen dance of creation. Each of us has the power to become a conduit for divine love, offering healing to a world that deeply needs it.

And as one spark ignites another, the **ripple effect** begins. A single act of alignment—be it a compassionate gesture or a bold step toward a dream—can set off waves of change far beyond what we can see. These ripples do not diminish as they travel; rather, they gather strength, carried by the interconnected field that binds us all. It's a reminder that no action aligned with the divine is ever too small. The energy we contribute to the collective weaves into a greater pattern, shaping the harmony of the whole.

**Service to the whole** is not a sacrifice but a fulfillment. When we align our actions with the needs of others, we discover the paradox of abundance: in giving, we receive. Each moment of selflessness draws us closer to the Creator, reaffirming our role as co-creators in the grand design. Whether we're supporting a cause, uplifting a friend, or simply holding space for another's journey, our service amplifies the resonance of unity.

**Quantum resonance** reveals the extraordinary potential of this alignment. Like musicians tuning to the same frequency, our collective energy creates harmonies that reverberate through the quantum field. By aligning with divine purpose, we become more than individuals; we become instruments in a cosmic symphony, amplifying vibrations that promote healing, peace, and transformation on a global scale.

The path of serving as a divine vessel asks not for perfection but for presence. It requires the willingness to act, even when the outcome remains unseen, and to trust the quantum field to magnify our aligned efforts. It invites us to embrace the mystery of how our small, sincere actions ripple outward, touching lives in ways we may never fully comprehend.

Yet, as profound as this calling is, it is also deeply personal. Each of us brings a unique note to the universal melody, and the Creator delights in the individuality of our contributions. It is in the interplay between our personal essence and the divine flow that the truest co-creation occurs.

•••

As we lean into the work of amplifying divine energy through our actions, a deeper truth emerges: this is not a one-time effort but an ongoing conversation with the Creator. Each ripple we send into the field, each moment of alignment, carries with it a response—an invitation to continue the dance.

In that exchange, we begin to see life not as a series of disconnected events but as part of an eternal dialogue, where every thought, action, and intention writes a new verse in the universal story.

# Chapter Thirteen

# The Eternal Dialogue: Co-Creation with the Divine

*"Prayer is not asking. It is a longing of the soul. It is daily admission of one's weakness. It is better in prayer to have a heart without words than words without a heart."*

— Mahatma Gandhi

Picture a storyteller weaving a tale so grand, so intricate, that every listener becomes a character within it. The plot twists with the choices they make, and each chapter unfolds as they step into their role. Now, consider this: what if that storyteller was the Creator and the story being told was the one you live every day? This is the essence of the eternal dialogue—a life lived as a co-author in a universal narrative, where every thought, action, and intention contributes to the unfolding story of creation.

Co-creation is not confined to extraordinary moments; it is woven into the fabric of our daily lives. By recognizing our place within a cosmic dialogue, we begin to see the sacred in the mundane and the extraordinary in the ordinary. Through this ongoing exchange, we align with divine order, uncover guidance in stillness, and trust the limitless potential of the quantum field.

## Cosmic Dialogue: Living as Part of a Universal Story

Life is not a series of disconnected events; it is an intricate story written in collaboration with the Creator. Each moment, whether marked by joy or challenge, is a verse in the song of existence. This cosmic dialogue is not reserved for the devout or the enlightened—it is available to all who pause to listen.

### The Language of the Universe

The universe speaks to us in subtle yet profound ways. A series of coincidences, a phrase in a song, or an unexpected encounter can often feel like whispers from something greater, nudging us toward a path we may not have considered. These are not random acts; they are threads in the tapestry of divine intention, woven with precision and care.

Consider the story of Dr. Eben Alexander, a neurosurgeon whose near-death experience during a coma challenged his scientific skepticism. In his journey to the brink of death, he encountered a vivid realm of connection and love, one that felt like an ongoing conversation with the Creator. His experience transformed his view of life, revealing that the universe is alive with intention and interaction.

### Your Role in the Story

In this universal story, we are both participants and co-authors. The Creator sets the stage and offers the inspiration, but we choose how to respond. It is a dance of free will and divine guidance, where every step we take shapes the narrative.

This truth can be both liberating and humbling. To realize that your choices ripple through the quantum field is to understand your immense power as a co-creator. Yet, it also invites responsibility—to act with intention, to align with love, and to trust that your story contributes to the greater good.

---

## Reflective Exercise: Finding Your Verse

Take a moment to reflect on the chapters of your life. What themes emerge? Are there moments that feel divinely guided, where the pieces seemed to fall into place? As you consider these questions, recognize that your story is not finished. Each new day offers an opportunity to write another verse, to align with the Creator's whispers, and step more fully into your role as a co-creator.

---

## Sacred Stillness: Finding Guidance in Quiet Moments

Amid the clamor of daily life, the voice of the Divine often speaks not in thunderous commands but in the gentle stillness that lies between breaths. It's in these quiet moments that the noise of the external world fades, leaving space for the whispers of insight, clarity, and divine guidance. Sacred stillness is where the dialogue with the Creator becomes intimate and profound, a sanctuary where answers arise without words.

## The Power of Silence

In a world brimming with distractions, silence can feel uncomfortable. Yet, it is in the silence that the quantum field hums its eternal song. Every great spiritual tradition recognizes the value of stillness—be it through meditation, prayer, or contemplative solitude. These practices are not merely rituals; they are doorways to a deeper awareness, a way to attune ourselves to the infinite wisdom that surrounds us.

Take the story of Thomas Merton, the Trappist monk who sought solitude in a hermitage. For Merton, silence was not an escape but an encounter. He once wrote of his experience in stillness as being immersed in "an immense sea of light and clarity." In that sacred quiet, he discovered a connection to the Divine that transformed not just his understanding of faith but his entire way of being.

## Stillness as a Portal to the Divine

Throughout history, sacred stillness has been the gateway to profound insights. The Buddha sat beneath the Bodhi tree in silent meditation and attained enlightenment. Jesus retreated to the wilderness to pray and reflect. These moments of stillness were not acts of withdrawal but of deep communion with the eternal.

Modern science echoes this ancient truth. Studies on mindfulness and meditation reveal that the brain's default mode network—the part associated with self-referential thoughts—quietens during periods of stillness. This allows for greater creativity, clarity, and connection to intuition. In essence, stillness opens the door to the quantum field, where inspiration and guidance flow freely.

### | *Stillness in Action: The Story of Malala Yousafzai* |

**Malala Yousafzai**, the youngest Nobel Peace Prize laureate, found clarity in the stillness of her recovery after surviving an attack by the Taliban. During the months of healing, far from the chaos of activism and school, she used the quiet moments to reconnect with her purpose. In interviews, she has spoken about the profound insights she gained during this time. The silence helped her see the bigger picture of her mission—advocating for the education of girls worldwide.

Her story exemplifies the transformative potential of stillness. Far from being passive, her quiet moments became the foundation for her renewed strength and vision, enabling her to amplify her voice and impact on a global scale.

---

## Stillness as a Portal to the Quantum Field

Physicists describe the quantum field as a realm of infinite potential, existing in a state of pure possibility until observed. Similarly, sacred stillness is a space where possibilities emerge—ideas take shape, insights crystallize, and pathways unfold. It is not an absence of activity but a profound state of receptivity, where the soul tunes in to the frequency of divine creation.

Consider how stillness works in nature. A seed lies dormant in the soil, appearing lifeless. Yet within its quiet form, potential stirs, waiting for the right moment to break forth into growth. Sacred stillness in our lives serves the same purpose. It nurtures our intentions and aligns them with divine timing, allowing them to grow into reality.

## Listening Beyond Words

Sacred stillness is not just about silence; it's about listening with the heart. It's the space where intuition blossoms, where answers arise without questions, and where the Creator's presence feels most immediate. This is not a passive state but an active communion, where we open ourselves to receive guidance, not as a demand but as a gift.

One businessman shared how, in the midst of a career crisis, he began setting aside ten minutes each morning for silent reflection. Over time, he found his mind clearing, and unexpected solutions began to emerge. He described it as "tuning into something greater," a way of accessing wisdom that seemed to flow from beyond his own understanding. That small act of stillness became his guiding compass.

---

## Reflective Exercise: Embracing the Quiet

Find a space where you can sit undisturbed for a few moments. Close your eyes and take slow, steady breaths. As your thoughts begin to settle, notice the stillness within you. Feel its depth, its expansiveness. Ask a question that has been on your heart, but do not seek an answer. Simply rest in the quiet and trust that clarity will come in time, not as a shout but as a gentle whisper.

---

Sacred stillness is not a retreat from life but an entry point into its fullest expression. It reminds us that the Creator is not a distant figure but an intimate presence, waiting to guide us when we are ready to listen.

## Why We Resist Stillness

Despite its power, stillness is often met with resistance. Our fast-paced world equates activity with progress, making quiet moments seem unproductive. Yet, the greatest breakthroughs often come not from doing but from being—from allowing the quantum field to work in ways we cannot predict or control.

The mind itself resists stillness, filling the void with thoughts, worries, and distractions. This is natural, but it is not insurmountable. Like any skill, cultivating stillness requires practice and patience. Even a few minutes a day can make a profound difference, creating space for the divine to speak into our lives.

## The Feedback Loop of Stillness and the Field

Sacred stillness is not a one-way conversation; it is a dialogue. As we quiet our minds, we become more attuned to the subtle feedback of the quantum field. This feedback often comes in the form of synchronicities, intuitive nudges, or a sudden sense of clarity. These moments remind us that the field is not passive—it is alive, responding to our energy and intentions.

A writer once described how she solved a creative block by stepping away from her desk and sitting quietly in her garden. She wasn't actively seeking a solution, but in the stillness, an idea surfaced—a simple, elegant resolution that had eluded her for weeks. She called it her "garden epiphany," a reminder that sometimes the best way to move forward is to pause.

## Practical Ways to Embrace Stillness

Stillness doesn't require a monastery or a mountain retreat. It can be found in the ordinary moments of life—a few quiet breaths before starting the day, a walk in nature without distractions, or simply sitting in a favorite chair with no agenda. The key is to approach these moments with openness, allowing the noise of the world to fade so that the voice of the Divine can be heard.

One simple practice is to focus on your breath. As you inhale, feel the air filling your lungs. As you exhale, release any tension or worry. With each breath, let your mind settle, like dust drifting to the bottom of a jar of water. In this stillness, you may find not just calm but clarity—a quiet knowing that guides your next step.

### | *Stillness and the Creative Field: Maya Angelou* |

**Maya Angelou,** the iconic poet and author, often spoke about her practice of retreating to a small, quiet space to write. She believed in the power of solitude, where she could listen to the "truths of the world" and channel them into her work. Angelou rented hotel rooms to escape distractions, turning these still spaces into creative sanctuaries.

Through these moments of intentional stillness, she wrote words that resonated across generations. Her practice demonstrates how quiet reflection connects us to the universal energy of creation, allowing us to express truths that transcend individual experience.

## The Gift of Sacred Stillness

Stillness is more than a practice; it is a gift we give ourselves. It is a reminder that we are not human doings but human beings, deeply connected to the source of all creation. In stillness, we find not just answers but also the courage to ask better questions, the strength to let go of what no longer serves us, and the wisdom to align our lives with divine purpose.

As the ancient poet Rumi said, *"Silence is the language of God; all else is poor translation."* In the quiet moments of our lives, we speak this sacred language, bridging the gap between the seen and the unseen, the known and the infinite.

In the sacred quiet, we find the wisdom of the quantum field—the still, small voice that reminds us we are never truly alone. Through stillness, we align with the Creator's intention, stepping into a co-creative relationship that unfolds in perfect harmony.

## Logos in Action: Applying Divine Order to Daily Life

### The Concept of Logos in Motion

Logos, the divine principle of reason and order, is not a relic of ancient philosophy; it is a living force woven into the fabric of daily existence. It is the thread of coherence that connects the stars in the heavens to the smallest details of our lives. When we align ourselves with Logos, we step into the flow of divine order, where clarity replaces confusion, and purpose drives every action.

Living with Logos means seeing life as a harmonious symphony, where even dissonant notes serve a greater composition. It invites us to act with intention, to make decisions rooted in wisdom, and to find the sacred in the mundane.

### | *Logos in Leadership: The Story of Angela Merkel* |

**Angela Merkel**, former Chancellor of Germany, is often celebrated for her calm and measured leadership style. Through some of the most turbulent times in European history—financial crises, refugee challenges, and a global pandemic—Merkel exemplified what it means to act in alignment with divine order.

Merkel's decisions were rarely impulsive. Instead, she approached challenges with deliberate thought and a commitment to long-term solutions. In interviews, she credited her background in physics with teaching her to respect the laws of nature and to recognize patterns of order amidst apparent chaos. By channeling this mindset into her leadership, Merkel became a stabilizing force, demonstrating how Logos can guide even the most complex human systems toward harmony.

### | *Logos in Social Justice: The Work of Bryan Stevenson* |

**Bryan Stevenson**, founder of the Equal Justice Initiative, has dedicated his life to seeking justice for the wrongly accused and marginalized. His approach to social justice reflects the essence of Logos—bringing balance and equity to a system often riddled with disorder and prejudice.

Stevenson speaks often about the importance of proximity—getting close to the people and communities most affected by injustice. This philosophy aligns with Logos, as it calls for a deep understanding of the interconnectedness of all life. His work, grounded in compassion and reason, has not only transformed individual lives but has also reshaped societal conversations about justice and humanity.

### | *Logos in Action: The Personal Story of Fred Rogers* |

Fred Rogers, known to millions as "Mister Rogers," lived a life that exemplified Logos. His work was not merely about children's television but about creating a space where kindness, understanding, and curiosity thrived. Each episode of Mister Rogers' Neighborhood was carefully crafted to reflect divine order—teaching children to navigate their emotions, embrace their individuality, and see the world through a lens of love.

Rogers once said, *"Deep and simple is far more essential than shallow and complex."* His words and actions mirrored the wisdom of Logos: simplicity that reveals profound truth and order that fosters growth and healing. Through his intentional living, Rogers demonstrated how everyday actions could align with the divine.

## The Science of Order in Chaos

Chaos theory, often seen as the antithesis of order, surprisingly reveals the presence of Logos in seemingly random systems. The patterns of a snowflake, the spirals of a galaxy, or the rhythm of heartbeats all reflect the divine principle of order within complexity. These natural phenomena remind us that, even in life's most chaotic moments, a deeper intelligence is at work, guiding outcomes toward balance and coherence.

## Practical Exercises for Living with Logos

Living in alignment with Logos begins with small, intentional actions. Start by examining one area of your life—relationships, work, or health—and ask: What does balance look like here? Take time to journal your thoughts, identifying habits or patterns that disrupt harmony.

Another practice is mindful decision-making. Before acting, pause and ask: Is this choice rooted in love and wisdom? Does it contribute to the greater good? These moments of reflection can transform ordinary actions into sacred expressions of divine order.

## | *Stories of Logos in Daily Life* |

Consider the story of **Chef José Andrés**, who founded World Central Kitchen to provide meals during disasters. His work, blending compassion with logistical precision, reflects Logos in action. Through his efforts, Andrés demonstrates that even in times of crisis, divine order can manifest through human ingenuity and love.

Or take the example of Malala Fund co-founder **Ziauddin Yousafzai**, who advocated for girls' education in Pakistan despite facing immense societal resistance. His unwavering commitment to equality and justice represents the alignment with divine principles that Logos invites us to embody.

## The Call of Logos

The stories of Angela Merkel, Bryan Stevenson, Fred Rogers, José Andrés, and Ziauddin Yousafzai illustrate that Logos is not an abstract ideal but a living force that guides us toward harmony and purpose. By aligning our actions with divine order, we become co-creators of a world that reflects the Creator's wisdom and love.

To live with Logos is to step into a sacred dialogue, where every choice becomes a note in the eternal symphony of existence. It is an invitation to act with intention, to find meaning in every moment, and to trust that divine order will always lead us home.

# Infinite Possibility: Trusting the Quantum Field to Support Co-Creation

## The Boundless Nature of Possibility

The quantum field is a canvas of infinite potential, waiting for intention and alignment to bring possibilities into form. It is a place where the improbable becomes reality, not by chance but through the deliberate interplay of thought, faith, and action. Trusting this field means embracing its unpredictability, knowing that its responses often exceed our expectations and defy our logic.

This trust is not passive resignation; it is active engagement. It is the courage to set intentions, take steps forward, and surrender the outcome to a greater intelligence—an intelligence that orchestrates galaxies yet cares deeply for the details of your life.

### | *Trust in the Unknown: The Story of Howard Schultz* |

**Howard Schultz**, the man who transformed Starbucks into a global coffee empire, provides a powerful example of trusting the quantum field. Growing up in a Brooklyn housing project, Schultz dreamed of something bigger but had no roadmap for success. Years later, while traveling through Italy, he experienced the warmth and culture of espresso bars. This vision ignited a passion to create something similar in the United States. Despite skepticism from investors and challenges in convincing Americans to embrace coffee culture, Schultz persisted. He trusted his vision and took bold actions to bring it to life. Today, Starbucks is a household name, proving that when you trust the field and act on inspired ideas, the universe responds in extraordinary ways.

---

## | *Stepping Forward: The Story of Misty Copeland* |

**Misty Copeland,** the first African American principal dancer with the American Ballet Theatre, trusted the quantum field to support her seemingly impossible dream. Starting ballet at a much later age than most dancers and facing societal and physical stereotypes, Copeland could have easily given up. But she embraced her unique journey and worked tirelessly, trusting that her dedication and passion would lead to something meaningful.

Her leap of faith was met with opportunities that aligned perfectly with her efforts. Today, she is not only a celebrated dancer but an inspiration to countless individuals, showing that trusting the unseen can defy limitations and redefine possibility.

---

## Practical Steps to Engage Infinite Potential

Begin by creating a vision that excites you—something that feels both inspiring and slightly beyond your reach. Write it down, speak it aloud, or meditate on it daily. Then, take small, purposeful actions toward that vision, trusting that each step sets ripples in motion.

Let go of the need to control every detail of the outcome. This surrender creates room for the quantum field to work in ways that surpass your expectations. Trust the field to fill in the gaps you cannot yet see, knowing that it operates with divine precision.

---

## The Interplay of Trust and Action

Trusting the quantum field does not mean standing still, waiting for miracles to happen. It means stepping forward with faith, even when the full picture is hidden. Trust and action work in tandem: one fuels the other, creating a dynamic flow that aligns you with the field's potential.

Consider the story of Wangari Maathai, the Kenyan environmentalist and

Nobel Peace Prize laureate. Maathai began her Green Belt Movement with the simple act of planting trees, aiming to combat deforestation and empower women. What started as a small initiative grew into a global movement, restoring ecosystems and inspiring millions. Maathai's trust in her vision, combined with her relentless action, allowed the quantum field to amplify her efforts in ways she could never have anticipated.

## The Science of Infinite Possibility

Quantum physics tells us that particles exist in a state of superposition until observed. This principle suggests that the universe holds countless possibilities at any given moment, and our attention collapses potential into reality. Trusting the quantum field means embracing this inherent abundance, knowing that every choice and intention carries the potential to shift your reality.

Neuroscience supports this idea as well. Studies on neuroplasticity reveal that focused thought can rewire the brain, creating new pathways for action and perception. By trusting your intentions and aligning them with positive action, you reshape not only your inner world but the external reality that mirrors it.

## | *Stories of Infinite Possibility in Action* |

The life of **Dr. Temple Grandin**, an animal behaviorist and advocate for autism awareness, is a testament to trusting the quantum field's potential. Diagnosed with autism at a time when little was understood about the condition, Grandin faced significant challenges. Yet her unique way of thinking became her greatest strength.

By embracing her perspective and pursuing her passion for animal welfare, Grandin revolutionized livestock handling, creating systems that are now industry standards. Her story highlights the power of trusting one's path, even when it defies conventional expectations, and allowing the quantum field to transform challenges into triumphs.

## An Invitation to Trust. A World Waiting to Be Created

Trusting the quantum field is an act of courage. It asks us to release control, embrace uncertainty, and believe in the unseen forces working on our behalf. Like Vera Rubin's discoveries, Steve Jobs' innovations, Wangari Maathai's movements, and Temple Grandin's breakthroughs, your life, too, is a story waiting to unfold. By trusting the field's infinite possibilities, you become a co-creator of a reality that reflects the divine wisdom woven into the universe.

From Schultz's espresso dreams to Copeland's ballet mastery, the quantum field reveals its boundless potential through lives transformed by trust and action. The field doesn't just respond to what you want; it amplifies the energy you invest in your vision. By trusting its unseen mechanisms and moving forward with purpose, you open yourself to infinite possibilities waiting to unfold.

## Revisiting the Core Concepts and Insights

Throughout this exploration, one truth emerges with radiant clarity: life is not a series of random events but a symphony of co-creation, played in harmony with the divine. The quantum field, vast and pulsating with infinite potential, is not a distant mystery. It is a constant companion, responding to every intention, belief, and action with profound precision. To embrace this truth is to step into a role of extraordinary responsibility and privilege: that of a co-creator.

The **dialogue** with the quantum field begins with awareness—recognizing that our thoughts and emotions ripple outward, shaping the world around us. Like waves meeting the shore, our intentions influence the unseen forces of the universe, returning as opportunities, synchronicities, and transformations. It is not enough to dream or wish; to manifest our desires, we must align belief, intention, and action in a unified flow. Trust becomes the bridge between possibility and reality, allowing the unseen to work in ways we may never fully understand.

Stories of transformation illuminate these truths with vivid brilliance. From the visionary entrepreneur who trusted her product to solve real-world problems, to the dancer who defied the odds through faith in her calling, the quantum field reveals itself in the lives of those willing to trust, act, and surrender. Such stories remind us that the divine doesn't only reside in lofty realms; it dances in our daily decisions, whispers through our **quiet moments**, and rises to meet us in our boldest aspirations.

To work with the quantum field is to embrace infinite possibility. This requires **letting go of control**—releasing the need to predict or manipulate outcomes—and instead stepping forward with trust. It is in this surrender that the greatest miracles often occur, as the field operates with a wisdom that transcends our own. Surrender is not passive; it is an active acknowledgment of partnership with the divine. By stepping into this partnership, we unlock doors to potential that we might never have opened on our own.

The field not only invites us to create for ourselves but to serve as conduits of creation for others. Through aligned action, we become vessels of divine energy, spreading ripples of well-being and inspiration into the collective. This isn't about grandeur or fame; it is about living each day with intention, knowing that even the smallest actions—when aligned with divine purpose—can have profound and far-reaching effects.

Science lends its voice to this spiritual understanding, confirming that the universe is an interconnected web of energy and potential. Concepts like quantum entanglement and superposition reveal a world where boundaries blur, where the smallest particle influences the vastness of creation. This scientific framework doesn't diminish the spiritual—it elevates it, providing a language through which we can articulate the mysteries of faith and co-creation.

The journey of co-creation is lifelong, unfolding one step, one intention, one moment of trust at a time. It requires courage to face the unknown, humility to listen to the whispers of the divine, and resilience to continue even when the path isn't clear. But as we engage in this process, we begin to see the beauty of life's unfolding—a beauty that is not merely given but co-created, shaped by our alignment with the field and the divine energy that infuses it.

...

This journey of infinite possibility invites us to reflect deeply on our heritage as divine co-creators. Each step forward reveals a new layer of truth, a new depth of connection. The quantum field, ever-responsive, whispers a timeless truth: we are not separate from the divine but integral to its unfolding story. Let us move forward with clarity, embracing the responsibility and wonder of reclaiming our role in this sacred dialogue. What lies ahead is the invitation to fully embody this truth and step into our divine heritage with trust, hope, and intention.

# Chapter Fourteen

# Reclaiming Our Divine Heritage

*"Act as if what you do makes a difference. It does."*
— William James

A seed holds the blueprint for an entire forest. Though tiny and unassuming, its potential is vast and waiting to be realized. So, too, within each of us lies a divine spark—an inherent connection to the infinite quantum field and the creative force of the universe. The question isn't whether this potential exists; the question is whether we will choose to awaken it.

This chapter is an invitation to step into the fullness of our divine heritage. By recognizing our interconnectedness, embracing the limitless possibilities of the quantum field, and aligning our lives with universal principles, we reclaim our role as co-creators in the grand design. This is not a distant goal or an abstract concept—it is a practical and transformative truth waiting to be realized in each moment.

## Recognizing Interconnectedness and Divine Unity

Our lives are woven into an intricate web of relationships, events, and energies. This interconnectedness is not merely poetic—it is a profound truth echoed by both ancient wisdom and modern science. Quantum entanglement reveals how particles separated by vast distances remain inexplicably connected, their states intertwined. This phenomenon is a reflection of a larger truth: we, too, are connected to every aspect of creation.

The ancient sages of many traditions spoke of this unity. In Eastern philosophies, the term "Indra's Net" describes the universe as a vast, jeweled net where every jewel reflects all others, symbolizing the interconnectedness of life. In modern terms, it's as if every thought, action, and intention sends ripples across the quantum field, touching the farthest reaches of existence.

## A Real-Life Connection

Think of the humanitarian Greg Mortenson, whose mission to build schools in remote regions of Pakistan and Afghanistan began with a single promise to a village elder. His journey illustrates how one person's actions—rooted in compassion and connection—can inspire global change. His story reminds us that we are not isolated beings but participants in a shared narrative where every choice contributes to the collective whole.

---

## Reflective Exercise: The Thread of Connection

Pause for a moment and reflect on the people, places, and events that have shaped your life. Trace the threads that connect them. How did a chance meeting lead to an opportunity? How did a single decision ripple outward, affecting those around you? As you consider these connections, recognize that the same web of unity links you to the divine source of all creation.

---

## The Spiritual Implication

To recognize our interconnectedness is to honor our role in the greater whole. It shifts our perspective from separation to unity, from isolation to belonging. When we see ourselves as part of the divine design, our actions take on new meaning, and our lives become a testament to the interconnected beauty of creation.

## Science Meets Spirit

The interconnectedness of life is not just a spiritual idea—it's a scientific reality. Quantum entanglement, ecological interdependence, and even the networks within our own brains mirror the unity that pervades the universe. Each breath we take is a reminder of this unity, as we exchange air with plants, animals, and the planet itself. This symphony of interdependence is a testament to the divine order that sustains all things.

Recognizing this interconnectedness is the first step in reclaiming our divine heritage. It opens our eyes to the truth that we are not separate from creation but intrinsic to it, co-creators in the unfolding story of the universe. From this awareness, the journey of co-creation begins—a journey rooted in unity, trust, and the infinite potential of the quantum field.

## Embracing the Infinite Potential of the Quantum Field

The quantum field is a realm of limitless possibility—a space where the rules of classical reality give way to boundless creativity. It is here that potential exists before it takes form, a blank canvas waiting for the brushstrokes of intention, belief, and trust. To embrace this field is to recognize that the only limits are those we place on ourselves.

### The Science of Infinite Potential

At its heart, quantum mechanics reveals a startling truth: particles exist in a state of superposition, embodying multiple possibilities until observed. In the same way, the quantum field holds infinite outcomes for our lives, each waiting to be "chosen" by the energy we project. This isn't magic—it's the interplay of consciousness and reality, a dance where our focus shapes the world around us.

Consider the double-slit experiment, where light behaves as both a particle and a wave depending on observation. This experiment illustrates the profound impact of intention. The act of observing transforms potential into reality. Similarly, when we align our thoughts and emotions with a clear vision, we draw possibilities from the field into tangible existence.

### | *Real-Life Inspiration: Vera Rubin's Vision* |

**Vera Rubin**, the pioneering astronomer who uncovered evidence of dark matter, serves as a testament to the power of embracing potential. In a field dominated by men, Rubin believed in the unseen forces of the universe long before they were acknowledged. Her groundbreaking research reshaped our understanding of cosmic structure. Rubin's unwavering trust in the unknown mirrors the quantum field itself: full of mysteries yet ready to reveal its secrets to those who approach it with curiosity and faith.

---

### The Role of Trust

Embracing the quantum field requires more than intellectual understanding—

it demands trust. Trust that the universe is abundant, that the field is responsive, and that even setbacks are part of the process. When we surrender our doubts and align with this potential, we become active participants in creation.

---

## Reflective Exercise: Stepping Into the Field

Take a moment to close your eyes and picture the quantum field as an infinite expanse of light and energy. Each point of light represents a possibility—some close, others far. Focus on one point, the one that aligns with your deepest desires. Hold it in your mind's eye, infusing it with belief and gratitude. Now, release it into the field, trusting that it will find its way into reality.

---

### The Gift of Possibility

Embracing infinite potential is both humbling and empowering. It reminds us that while we cannot control every outcome, we can influence the flow of creation. By aligning our intentions with the quantum field, we invite opportunities, synchronicities, and solutions that might otherwise remain hidden.

### The Spiritual Dimension

The quantum field is not only a wellspring of possibility but also a reflection of divine abundance. It is the Creator's gift, a reminder that we are never truly limited, even when circumstances seem constrained. Each time we align with this truth, we draw closer to our divine heritage, stepping into the role of co-creators.

Through the lens of the quantum field, life becomes an adventure—a journey of discovery where every possibility is waiting to be explored. With trust, intention, and alignment, we transform the infinite into the tangible, bringing the unseen into the seen and the potential into the real.

## P Living Intentionally and in Alignment with Universal Order

To live intentionally is to act as though every thought, every decision, and every action carries weight in the great symphony of existence. It is an acknowledgment that our lives, far from being isolated or random, are deeply woven into the fabric of the universe. Universal order is not a distant concept; it is the rhythm we feel when we pause, listen, and align ourselves with the energy that flows through all creation.

## The Power of Intentional Living

Intentional living begins with awareness—awareness of the choices we make, the energy we emit, and the impact we leave behind. Every moment offers a chance to decide what kind of ripple we wish to send into the quantum field. Whether it's a kind word, a deliberate pause, or a focused effort, each act carries the power to create, heal, and transform.

Consider the story of Malala Yousafzai. When she was just a young girl in Pakistan, she recognized the injustice of educational barriers for girls. Despite immense danger, she chose to speak out, not with anger or chaos, but with clarity and intention. Her courage sparked a global movement, not because she sought fame, but because her actions aligned with a higher universal principle: the belief in the dignity and equality of all. Malala's story exemplifies how one individual, living intentionally, can resonate with the collective consciousness and inspire profound change.

## Recognizing Universal Patterns

From the spirals of galaxies to the veins of a leaf, nature reveals a profound order that connects all life. These patterns—reflected in sacred geometry, natural cycles, and even human behavior—are not coincidental. They are evidence of a universal intelligence that governs creation. By living intentionally, we align ourselves with this order, stepping into harmony with the forces that sustain existence.

For example, think of an architect designing a bridge. The structure must respect the natural laws of physics and the environment it inhabits. In the same way, our lives must respect the universal principles of balance, reciprocity, and growth. When we live in alignment with these principles, we create strength and stability, not just for ourselves but for all we touch.

### | *Real-Life Story: Chadwick Boseman's Purposeful Path* |

**Chadwick Boseman**, the late actor known for his transformative roles, approached his work with profound intentionality. Despite battling a private fight with cancer, he chose roles that elevated stories of resilience, justice, and empowerment. He understood that his craft was more than entertainment—it was a vehicle for meaning and change. His portrayal of King T'Challa in *Black Panther* became a cultural milestone, reflecting a vision of dignity and possibility for millions. Boseman's life reminds us that intentionality is not about perfection; it's about showing up with purpose, even in the face of challenges.

---

### The Daily Practice of Alignment

Living in alignment requires regular reflection. Are your actions consistent with your values? Are your thoughts and emotions contributing to the life you want to create? Alignment doesn't mean eliminating difficulties; it means approaching them with a sense of purpose and trust in universal order.

---

### Reflective Exercise: Creating a Daily Intention

Begin each day by setting a simple intention. Take a moment to breathe deeply and ask yourself: "What energy do I want to bring into today?" Whether it's kindness, focus, or patience, carry that intention as a touchstone. Throughout the day, notice when you're in harmony with that energy and when you're not. Gently realign yourself, knowing that every adjustment strengthens your connection to the greater whole.

---

### Spiritual Insights into Alignment

In spiritual traditions, alignment often begins with surrender—not in defeat, but in trust. To surrender is to acknowledge that while we can steer our ship, the currents of the universe guide us. This surrender does not diminish our power; it amplifies it as we align with forces far greater than ourselves.

Living intentionally and in alignment is both an art and a discipline. It asks us to trust the unseen, to act with purpose, and to embrace the interconnectedness of all things. By doing so, we not only transform our own lives but contribute to the harmony of the collective. And as the quantum field reflects, even the smallest shift in alignment can send waves of creation through the cosmos.

## Starting the Journey of Co-Creation with Hope and Trust

Stepping into the role of a co-creator is not a one-time decision; it is a continuous act of hope, courage, and faith. It's the quiet confidence that the vast unknown—the quantum field—is a space of infinite potential waiting to partner with us. Yet, to engage fully in this sacred dance, we must take the first step with an open heart and unwavering trust.

## Trusting the Unseen

Starting the journey of co-creation begins with relinquishing the need for certainty. We are conditioned to seek assurance, to crave proof before we act. But co-creation requires a different approach: acting with the faith that the quantum field will respond, even when the path ahead seems uncertain.

### | *Real-Life Story: Canadian Astronaut* |

Consider the story of Colonel Chris Hadfield, the Canadian astronaut whose journey to space began not with guarantees but with a dream he trusted despite the odds. From a young age, Hadfield envisioned himself walking in space, even though Canada had no space program at the time. With trust in his vision and a relentless commitment to preparation, he became one of the world's most celebrated astronauts. His story demonstrates that trust in the unseen often leads to extraordinary outcomes.

---

## Small Steps, Big Ripples

Co-creation doesn't demand monumental actions from the start. It begins with the smallest gestures—writing a journal entry, planting a seed of intention, or simply voicing gratitude for what is yet to come. These acts, though modest, resonate through the quantum field, signaling our readiness to engage. A gardener planting seeds does so not with certainty but with faith in the unseen forces of nature to nurture and grow what's been planted. Similarly, our small, deliberate actions in the quantum field set the stage for growth beyond what we can initially perceive.

Take the example of Brandon Stanton, the creator of Humans of New York. What began as a simple project to photograph and document stories of strangers in New York City grew into a global phenomenon. Stanton trusted in the impact of sharing these narratives, even when he didn't know where the project might lead. By starting small and staying aligned with his purpose, he created a movement that touched millions of lives.

## The Role of Resilience

Starting a journey with hope and trust often comes with challenges. Doubts creep in, and obstacles appear where we least expect them. Yet, it is our resilience—the determination to keep moving forward despite setbacks—that ensures the journey continues. Oprah Winfrey's rise from poverty and adversity to global influence is a powerful testament to this truth. Her resilience, coupled with her unwavering belief in her purpose, allowed her to overcome unimaginable odds and inspire others to trust their own paths.

---

## Reflective Exercise: Embracing the First Step

Pause for a moment and consider something you've hesitated to begin—a project, a dream, or even a conversation. Write it down, not with the intention of solving it immediately, but simply to acknowledge it. Then, close your eyes, take a deep breath, and visualize yourself taking the first step. What would that look like? How would it feel? Release any pressure to have all the answers. Trust that the field will respond when you act.

---

### Co-Creation as a Leap of Faith

Beginning the journey is often less about knowing and more about trusting. It's about taking that leap of faith, assured that the universe will rise to meet us halfway. When Dr. Martin Luther King Jr. said, *"Faith is taking the first step even when you don't see the whole staircase,"* he encapsulated the spirit of co-creation. Each step forward is a declaration of trust in the process, a vote of confidence in the field's capacity to align and amplify our intentions.

Through hope and trust, we bridge the gap between possibility and reality. Each step, no matter how small, sets the quantum field into motion, creating ripples that echo across the vast expanse of potential. The journey of co-creation begins not with certainty but with a simple act of belief—an act that holds the power to change everything.

## Revisiting the Core Concepts and Insights

The journey of reclaiming our divine heritage invites us to see the universe not as a collection of separate parts but as a unified whole, alive with infinite potential. It's an understanding that begins with recognizing the threads of interconnectedness binding all existence, a truth whispered by ancient wisdom and echoed by modern quantum science. Each action, thought, and intention we bring into the world reverberates through this cosmic web, influencing not just our individual lives but the harmony of the greater symphony.

**Divine unity** is not a concept reserved for sacred texts or spiritual leaders; it's a reality accessible to each of us when we step back and see ourselves as integral parts of the universal dance. When we embrace this oneness, the boundaries between "self" and "other" dissolve. We begin to understand that what we do for another, we ultimately do for ourselves. This recognition calls us to live with compassion, to act with purpose, and to align with the higher order that governs existence.

The **quantum field**, an invisible reservoir of energy and possibility, holds a blueprint for infinite creation. When we embrace its potential, we begin to see life not as a series of random occurrences but as a playground of intentionality. The field responds to the vibrations we send—our thoughts, feelings, and actions— amplifying those aligned with love, gratitude, and purpose. Like a musician tuning their instrument to match the orchestra, we too must align our frequencies with the symphony of the universe to co-create our highest vision.

**Intentionality is** the compass that guides us. Without it, our lives can drift like leaves in the wind, moved by external forces rather than inner purpose. Yet, with clarity of intention, even the smallest acts become imbued with significance. A kind word, a journal entry, or a single step toward a dream sends ripples through the field, creating possibilities we may not yet see. As history and science have shown, alignment with clear intentions can unlock doors thought to be forever closed.

To **co-create** effectively, we must also confront the barriers within ourselves— the fears, doubts, and limiting beliefs that keep us tethered to old ways of being. It's not enough to hope for change; we must actively cultivate the mindset and habits that allow us to step into alignment with divine order. Trust becomes our anchor here, for true creation often requires stepping into the unknown, trusting that the ground will appear beneath our feet.

Hope and trust are the cornerstones of co-creation. They remind us that we don't need all the answers to begin; we simply need the courage to take the first step. Whether that step is as simple as voicing a dream aloud or as challenging as overcoming deeply rooted self-doubt, each act of faith moves the quantum field into motion. The stories of those who have walked this path before us—individuals who defied the odds to bring their visions to life—serve as reminders of what's possible when trust replaces fear.

Living intentionally also calls for alignment with universal order. This is not a rigid system but a harmonious balance—a flow we tap into when we act with purpose and authenticity. Living in alignment means recognizing that every choice matters, every thought carries weight, and every moment holds the power to redirect our trajectory. It is through this conscious alignment that we create not just for ourselves but for the collective, contributing to a greater harmony that uplifts all.

To reclaim our divine heritage is to step boldly into this co-creative role, knowing that the field is alive with infinite potential and ready to respond. It is to live with the understanding that we are not separate from the divine but active participants in its expression.

And as we take each step with faith, hope, and trust, we begin to see that the greatest creation of all is the life we shape with our own hands.

# The Infinite Canvas of Co-Creation

*"You don't have to see the whole staircase,
just take the first step."*

— Martin Luther King Jr.

Life is a masterpiece, a constantly unfolding creation shaped not only by what we do but by who we choose to be. Each thought, action, and intention is a brushstroke on the infinite canvas of the quantum field, forming the portrait of your reality. Along this journey, you've explored the profound connection between science and spirituality, seen glimpses of divine design, and discovered tools to align your energy with the boundless possibilities of creation. Now, as this book comes to an end, the real work begins—bringing these insights into your daily life and weaving them into the fabric of your existence.

The most profound truth of all is that you are not a passive observer of life. You are an active participant, a co-creator. The quantum field isn't a distant, abstract concept—it's an extension of your being, responding to the energy you emit and reflecting it back in the form of experiences, relationships, and opportunities. Every moment is an invitation to step into this creative role with greater awareness and intentionality.

## The Power of Awareness and Alignment

Throughout this journey, a single thread has connected every concept, practice, and story: alignment. When your thoughts, emotions, and actions resonate with your highest intentions, you harmonize with the divine flow of the universe. This is where transformation occurs—not through force or manipulation, but through a quiet, powerful alignment with the energies that create worlds.

Awareness is the first step. By becoming conscious of your thoughts and recognizing how they shape your reality, you open the door to possibility. The quantum field does not judge or discriminate; it simply reflects the frequencies you send. If your energy is filled with doubt, fear, or negativity, those vibrations will echo back. But when you anchor yourself in love, gratitude, and purpose, you send ripples of creation that attract the life you truly desire.

This is not about perfection. You don't have to get it right every time. Life will always present challenges, moments of uncertainty, and opportunities for growth. What matters is how you respond—whether you choose to align with fear or trust, scarcity or abundance, resistance or flow. Each decision shapes not only your personal journey but the larger symphony of creation.

## The Sacred Dance of Intention and Action

Intention without action is like a seed never planted. The quantum field is activated by movement—by the choices you make, the steps you take, and the energy you invest in your dreams. This doesn't mean you must strive or struggle; rather, it means you must participate in the process of creation with faith and determination.

Think of the farmer who plants seeds, tends to the soil, and waters the crops. They cannot force the sun to shine or the rain to fall, but they trust the natural order to do its part. So it is with co-creation. Your role is to show up, to take inspired action, and to trust the field to meet you halfway. The magic lies not in controlling the outcome but in surrendering to the flow while doing your part with clarity and purpose.

Reflect on the practices you've learned: journaling to clarify your intentions, visualization to align your energy, gratitude to amplify resonance, and mindfulness to stay present in the now. Each practice is a tool, a way of nurturing the soil of your life so that your intentions can take root and flourish.

## Trusting the Process

Faith is the foundation of all creation. It is the bridge between intention and manifestation, the quiet knowing that the field is always working in your favor, even when you cannot yet see the results. Trust is not passive; it is an active choice to believe in possibilities beyond what the eye can see.

When doubts creep in, as they inevitably will, return to this truth: the universe is infinitely creative and always conspiring for your growth and highest good. Trust does not mean you will never face obstacles or challenges, but it does mean you will see them for what they are—stepping stones on the path to your greatest unfolding. Even setbacks hold the potential to redirect you toward something more aligned with your true purpose.

Faith also invites you to embrace the unknown. The quantum field operates in ways that defy linear thinking, often delivering outcomes that exceed anything you could have planned or predicted. When you release the need for control and allow the field to do its work, you make space for miracles to unfold.

## Embracing Your Divine Heritage

At the heart of this journey is the understanding that you are not separate from the divine. You are a vessel for its energy, a reflection of its infinite creativity, and an integral part of its expression. Reclaiming your divine heritage means stepping fully into this truth, not as a concept but as a lived experience.

When you see yourself as a co-creator, you begin to move through life with a sense of purpose and empowerment. You realize that every interaction, every choice, and every moment is an opportunity to contribute to the greater harmony of existence. Your life becomes a sacred offering, a way of channeling divine energy into the world for the benefit of all.

This perspective shifts how you approach challenges, relationships, and even your own limitations. Instead of seeing obstacles as barriers, you begin to see them as invitations to grow. Instead of seeking validation or approval from others, you find it within yourself, knowing that you are already whole. And instead of fearing failure, you embrace it as part of the creative process—a necessary step on the path to mastery.

## A Call to Action

The path of co-creation is not a destination but a lifelong practice. It is a journey of discovery, growth, and continual alignment with the divine energy that flows through you. As you step forward, remember that you are not alone. The field is always with you, guiding you, responding to you, and supporting your highest vision.

So what will you create? What dreams will you bring to life? What impact will you make on the world around you? These are not questions to ponder passively; they are calls to action. Take what you have learned and put it into practice. Begin with small steps—a journal entry, a moment of gratitude, a single act of kindness—and let those steps lead to bigger shifts.

And when you stumble, as everyone does, know that you can always return to the field. It is never too late to realign, to begin again, and to step back into the flow of creation. The universe is patient, generous, and infinitely forgiving, always ready to meet you where you are.

## Looking Ahead

This book is not the end of your journey; it is the beginning. The insights and practices you've explored here are tools, not answers—guides to help you navigate the unfolding mystery of life. As you move forward, you will continue to learn, grow, and deepen your connection to the quantum field. New questions will arise, new challenges will appear, and new possibilities will unfold. Embrace them all as part of the sacred dance of co-creation.

If you seek further guidance, resources are available to support you on this path. Whether through additional reading, workshops, or communities of like-minded individuals, you will find companions for the journey. But remember, the greatest resource of all is within you—the spark of divinity that connects you to the infinite.

And now, as you turn the final page, take a moment to reflect on the life you wish to create. Hold that vision in your heart, not as a distant dream but as a reality already in motion. Trust the field to guide you, take inspired action, and know that the universe is conspiring in your favor.

You are a co-creator, a vessel for divine energy, and a participant in the grand symphony of existence.


Go forth with faith, hope, and trust—let the masterpiece of your life unfold.

# Suggested Reading: Unlocking Deeper Understanding

The journey through *Quantum Whispers: A Journey Into Co-Creation, Where Science Meets Spirit and Possibilities Are Infinite,* is one of exploration—melding the boundaries of science, spirituality, and human potential. To enrich this journey, I've compiled a list of ten books that expand upon the themes explored in these pages. These works are widely regarded as classics or foundational texts, celebrated for their recognition in academic, spiritual, and scientific circles, as well as their enduring influence on readers and researchers in relevant fields.

Each of these books offers unique insights, whether through groundbreaking scientific discoveries, profound philosophical musings, or practical tools for personal transformation. They bridge disciplines, connect ideas, and illuminate paths for understanding the mysteries of the universe—and our place within it. From quantum theory to metaphysics and from cosmic mysteries to the intricacies of the human mind, these books invite you to go deeper, think broader, and embrace the infinite possibilities of co-creation.

As you dive into these works, you may find threads of familiarity woven through them—concepts and ideas touched upon in this book—but explored in richer detail and from different perspectives. Let these books be your companions as you continue this journey of discovery, aligning your curiosity with the ever-expanding boundaries of what is possible.

## The Top 10 Recommended Books

*The Tao of Physics: An Exploration of the Parallels Between Modern Physics and Eastern Mysticism* by Fritjof Capra. A classic that bridges the gap between modern science and ancient spiritual wisdom.

*The Holographic Universe* by Michael Talbot. A groundbreaking exploration of how the universe may operate as a hologram, mirroring quantum and spiritual principles.

*The Field: The Quest for the Secret Force of the Universe* by Lynne McTaggart. A compelling deep dive into the quantum field and its implications for human consciousness and interconnectedness.

*Wholeness and the Implicate Order* by David Bohm. A profound philosophical and scientific exploration of the interconnected fabric of reality.

*The Fabric of the Cosmos: Space, Time, and the Texture of Reality* by Brian Greene. An accessible yet profound explanation of the nature of space, time, and the universe.

*Breaking the Habit of Being Yourself: How to Lose Your Mind and Create a New One* by Joe Dispenza. A practical guide to rewiring your brain and aligning with the quantum field to create transformative change.

*Think and Grow Rich* by Napoleon Hill. A timeless classic on the power of intention, visualization, and mindset in shaping reality.

*Healing Sounds: The Power of Harmonics* by Jonathan Goldman. An exploration of sound and vibration as tools for healing and alignment with universal energy.

*The Power of Now: A Guide to Spiritual Enlightenment* by Eckhart Tolle. A transformative guide to living in the present moment, where all possibilities reside.

*Becoming Supernatural: How Common People Are Doing the Uncommon* by Joe Dispenza. A follow-up to Dispenza's earlier work, blending quantum principles with practical tools for transformation.

These books provide a blend of scientific rigor and spiritual insight, offering a well-rounded foundation for understanding the quantum field, consciousness, and co-creation.

## Complete List of Books for Further Study

### Quantum Physics and the Universe

*The Tao of Physics: An Exploration of the Parallels Between Modern Physics and Eastern Mysticism* by Fritjof Capra

*The Holographic Universe* by Michael Talbot

*The Fabric of the Cosmos: Space, Time, and the Texture of Reality* by Brian Greene

*Wholeness and the Implicate Order* by David Bohm

*Quantum Reality: Beyond the New Physics* by Nick Herbert

## Consciousness and Mind-Body Connection

*The Field: The Quest for the Secret Force of the Universe* by Lynne McTaggart

*The Brain That Changes Itself* by Norman Doidge

*How God Changes Your Brain: Breakthrough Findings from a Leading Neuroscientist* by Andrew Newberg and Mark Robert Waldman

*Healing Sounds: The Power of Harmonics* by Jonathan Goldman

*Mindfulness: An Eight-Week Plan for Finding Peace in a Frantic World* by Mark Williams and Danny Penman

## Spirituality and Transformation

*How to Know God: The Soul's Journey into the Mystery of Mysteries* by Deepak Chopra

*The Seat of the Soul* by Gary Zukav

*Sacred Geometry: Philosophy and Practice* by Robert Lawlor

*The Power of Now: A Guide to Spiritual Enlightenment* by Eckhart Tolle

*Cosmos and Psyche: Intimations of a New World View* by Richard Tarnas

## The Science of Manifestation and Co-Creation

*Think and Grow Rich* by Napoleon Hill

*Breaking the Habit of Being Yourself: How to Lose Your Mind and Create a New One* by Joe Dispenza

*Ask and It Is Given: Learning to Manifest Your Desires* by Esther and Jerry Hicks

*The Secret* by Rhonda Byrne

*Becoming Supernatural: How Common People Are Doing the Uncommon* by Joe Dispenza

## Energetics and Resonance

*Vibrational Medicine: The #1 Handbook of Subtle-Energy Therapies* by Richard Gerber

*The Healing Power of Sound: Recovery from Life-Threatening Illness Using Sound, Voice, and Music* by Mitchell L. Gaynor

*Energy Medicine: The Science and Mystery of Healing* by Jill Blakeway

*The HeartMath Solution: The Institute of HeartMath's Revolutionary Program for Engaging the Power of the Heart's Intelligence* by Doc Childre and Howard Martin

*The Body Electric: Electromagnetism and the Foundation of Life* by Robert O. Becker and Gary Selden

# Bibliography

Achterberg, J. (1985). *Imagery in healing: Shamanism and modern medicine.* Shambhala Publications.

Aspect, A., Grangier, P., & Roger, G. (1982). Experimental tests of realistic local theories via Bell's theorem. *Physical Review Letters, 49*(2), 91–94. https://doi.org/10.1103/PhysRevLett.49.91

Barrow, J. D., & Tipler, F. J. (1986). *The anthropic cosmological principle.* Oxford University Press.

Bascomb, N. (2004). *The Perfect Mile: Three Athletes, One Goal, and Less Than Four Minutes to Achieve It.* Houghton Mifflin Harcourt.

Bekenstein, J. D. (2003). Information in the holographic universe. *Scientific American, 289*(2), 58–65.

Benedetti, F., Carlino, E., & Pollo, A. (2004). How placebos change the patient's brain. *Neuropsychopharmacology, 29*(2), 339–354.

Bohm, D. (1980). *Wholeness and the implicate order.* Routledge.

Byrne, R. (2006). *The secret.* Atria Books.

Capra, F. (1975). *The Tao of physics: An exploration of the parallels between modern physics and Eastern mysticism.* Shambhala.

Capra, F. (1996). *The web of life: A new scientific understanding of living systems.* Anchor Books.

Chopra, D. (2000). *How to know God: The soul's journey into the mystery of mysteries.* Harmony Books.

Couzin, I. D., Krause, J., Franks, N. R., & Levin, S. A. (2005). Effective leadership and decision-making in animal groups on the move. *Nature, 433*(7025), 513–516.

Doidge, N. (2007). *The brain that changes itself: Stories of personal triumph from the frontiers of brain science.* Penguin Books.

Einstein, A., Podolsky, B., & Rosen, N. (1935). Can quantum-mechanical description of physical reality be considered complete? *Physical Review, 47*(10), 777–780.

Emmons, R. A., & McCullough, M. E. (2003). Counting blessings versus burdens: An experimental investigation of gratitude and subjective well-being in daily life. *Journal of Personality and Social Psychology, 84*(2), 377–389.

Freeman, K. (1948). *Ancilla to the Pre-Socratic philosophers: A complete translation of the fragments in Diels, Fragmente der Vorsokratiker.* Harvard University Press.

Gleick, J. (1987). *Chaos: Making a new science.* Viking Penguin.

Greene, B. (2004). *The fabric of the cosmos: Space, time, and the texture of reality.* Alfred A. Knopf.

Gross, J. J. (2015). Emotion regulation: Current status and future prospects. *Psychological Inquiry, 26*(1), 1-26.

Goldman, J. (2002). *Healing sounds: The power of harmonics.* Inner Traditions.

HeartMath Institute. (2012). Heart coherence research. *HeartMath.org.*

Hameroff, S. R., & Penrose, R. (1996). Orchestrated reduction of quantum coherence in brain microtubules: A model for consciousness. *Journal of Consciousness Studies, 3*(1), 36-53.

Heisenberg, W. (1958). *Physics and philosophy: The revolution in modern science.* Harper & Row.

Hill, N. (1937). *Think and grow rich.* The Ralston Society.

Hollingsworth, J. C., Ashton, C. M., & Wray, N. P. (2002). A controlled trial of arthroscopic surgery for osteoarthritis of the knee. *New England Journal of Medicine, 347*(2), 81-88.

John 1:1–5. (n.d.). *The Holy Bible: King James Version.*

Kabat-Zinn, J. (1990). *Full catastrophe living: Using the wisdom of your body and mind to face stress, pain, and illness.* Bantam Dell.

Kafatos, M., & Nadeau, R. (2000). *The conscious universe: Parts and wholes in physical reality.* Springer.

Langer, E. J. (1989). *Mindfulness.* Addison-Wesley.

Laszlo, E. (2007). *Science and the Akashic field: An integral theory of everything.* Inner Traditions.

Lawlor, R. (1989). *Sacred geometry: Philosophy and practice.* Thames & Hudson.

LeDoux, J. (1998). *The Emotional Brain: The Mysterious Underpinnings of Emotional Life.* Simon & Schuster.

Le Scouarnec, R. P., Poirier, R. M., Owens, J. E., Gauthier, J., Taylor, A. G., & Foresman, P. A. (2001). Use of binaural beat tapes for treatment of anxiety: A pilot study of tape preference and outcomes. *Alternative Therapies in Health and Medicine, 7*(1), 58–63.

Leggett, A. J. (2002). Testing the limits of quantum mechanics: Motivation, state of play, prospects. *Journal of Physics: Condensed Matter, 14*(15), R415.

Matthew 13:31–32. (n.d.). *The Holy Bible: King James Version.*

McCraty, R., Atkinson, M., & Tomasino, D. (2004). Modulation of DNA by coherent heart frequencies. *Institute of HeartMath Research Center.*

McCraty, R., Atkinson, M., & Bradley, R. T. (2015). Electrophysiological evidence of intuition: Part 1. The surprising role of the heart. *Journal of Alternative and Complementary Medicine, 21*(5), 275–286.

McEvilley, T. (2002). *The shape of ancient thought: Comparative studies in Greek and Indian philosophies.* Allworth Press.

McTaggart, L. (2008). *The field: The quest for the secret force of the universe.* HarperCollins.

Moseley, J. B., O'Malley, K., Petersen, N. J., Menke, T. J., Brody, B. A., Kuykendall, D. H., Hollingsworth, J. C., Ashton, C. M., & Wray, N. P. (2002). A controlled trial of arthroscopic surgery for osteoarthritis of the knee. *New England Journal of Medicine,* 347(2), 81–88. https://doi.org/10.1056/NEJMoa013259

Neary, L. (2017). J.K. Rowling: A biography. *The New Yorker.* Retrieved from www.newyorker.com.

Newberg, A., & Waldman, M. R. (2009). *How God changes your brain: Breakthrough findings from a leading neuroscientist.* Ballantine Books.

Orme-Johnson, D. W., et al. (1988). International peace project in the Middle East: The effect of the Maharishi technology of the unified field. *Journal of Conflict Resolution, 32*(4), 776–812.

Pennebaker, J. W., & Seagal, J. D. (1999). Forming a story: The health benefits of narrative. *Journal of Clinical Psychology, 55*(10), 1243–1254.

Penrose, R., & Hameroff, S. R. (2011). Consciousness in the universe: Neuroscience, quantum space-time geometry, and Orch-OR theory. *Physics of Life Reviews, 11*(1), 39-78.

Phelps, M., & Abrahamson, A. (2016). *Beneath the surface: My story.* Sports Publishing.

Radhakrishnan, S. (1953). *The principal Upanishads.* HarperCollins.

Rubik, B. (2002). The biofield hypothesis: Its biophysical basis and role in medicine. *Journal of Alternative and Complementary Medicine, 8*(6), 703–717.

Ryan, R. M., & Deci, E. L. (2000). Self-determination theory and the facilitation of intrinsic motivation, social development, and well-being. *American Psychologist, 55*(1), 68-78.

Ryff, C. D., & Singer, B. (1998). The contours of positive human health. *Psychological Inquiry, 9*(1), 1–28.

Schumann, W. O. (1952). Über die strahlungslosen Eigenschwingungen einer leitenden Kugel, die von einer Luftschicht und einer Ionosphärenhülle umgeben ist. *Zeitschrift für Naturforschung A, 7*(3), 149–154.

Schrödinger, E. (1935). Die gegenwärtige Situation in der Quantenmechanik. *Naturwissenschaften, 23*(48), 807-812.

Schwartz, J. M., Stapp, H. P., & Beauregard, M. (2005). Quantum physics in neuroscience and psychology: A neurophysical model of mind-brain interaction. *Philosophical Transactions of the Royal Society B: Biological Sciences, 360*(1458), 1309–1327. https://doi.org/10.1098/rstb.2004.1598

Seligman, M. E. P., Steen, T. A., Park, N., & Peterson, C. (2005). Positive psychology progress: Empirical validation of interventions. *American Psychologist, 60*(5), 410–421.

Stewart, I. (2001). *Nature's numbers: The unreal reality of mathematics.* Basic Books.

Tarnas, R. (2006). *Cosmos and psyche: Intimations of a new world view.* Viking Penguin.

Taylor, S. E., & Pham, L. B. (1996). Why thinking about goals and actions is not enough: The role of mental simulation. *Psychological Bulletin, 120*(3), 328–355.

Tillich, P. (1951). *Systematic theology, Vol. 1.* University of Chicago Press.

Wheeler, J. A. (1983). Law without law. In J. A. Wheeler & W. H. Zurek (Eds.), *Quantum theory and measurement.* Princeton University Press.

Wheeler, J. A. (1984). Delayed-choice experiments and the nature of reality. *Foundations of Physics, 14*(10), 801-825.

Wheeler, J. A. (1990). Information, physics, quantum: The search for links. In *Complexity, entropy, and the physics of information.* Addison-Wesley.

Zohar, D., & Marshall, I. (2000). *Spiritual intelligence: The ultimate intelligence.* Bloomsbury Publishing.